Crossroads
The Politics of Reform and Repression
1976 – 1986

Crossroads

The Politics of Reform and Repression
1976 – 1986

Josette Cole

Ravan Press  Johannesburg

To the memory of Edith — my mother

Published by Ravan Press (Pty) Ltd
P O Box 31134, Braamfontein,
Johannesburg, 2017
South Africa

First published 1987

ISBN 0 86975 318 5

Cover design by Carl Becker
Cover photograph courtesy of Dave Hartman
Set in 10 on 12pt English Times
Printed by Galvin and Sales Cape Town

Contents

Acknowledgements

In the course of a number of years conceptualising and, eventually, writing this book, I have become indebted to many people whose help was crucial to this process. It is unfortunately not possible here to thank the countless colleagues and friends who contributed, but I would like to name just a few whose assistance deserves special mention. First and foremost are the residents of Old Crossroads, New Crossroads and the former satellite communities, all of whom shared with me the stories of their lives in the midst of ongoing crises. In the course of my fieldwork and research they shared more with me than they will ever know — perhaps nobody more so than my long-time colleague and friend Regina Ntongana.

In writing the original thesis, a substantial part of which is included in this book, as well as this study, I was assisted and inspired by a number of individuals and organisations. Special thanks are due to members of the History and Economic History Departments (UCT), especially to my supervisor and editor Maureen Swan. I owe much to her for her encouragement, constructive criticism, editorial advice, and the many hours she spent discussing the work with me. Neither the original thesis, nor this book, could have materialised without her. I am also grateful to Virginia Zweigenthal, a loyal and dear friend, who inspired me to persevere at times when my own intellectual and physical stamina was visibly on the wane, and who spent countless hours doing the fiddly technical and editing tasks for which I had long lost patience. Thanks are also due to Laurine Platzky, a long-time colleague and friend who, over the past decade, consistently supported my work in, and on, Crossroads. I am also grateful to local friends, as well as others from various parts of the world, all of whom influenced my thinking and contributed to my understanding of social reality. The Surplus People Project, Western Cape Committee, which released me from my regular fieldwork duties at the end of 1986 in order to complete the manuscript, also deserves special mention.

The financial support for my original study (1985-1986) came from the Human Sciences Research Council and the Harry Oppenheimer Trust, Centre for African Studies, University of Cape Town.

For the photographs reproduced in the book, I am grateful to two sources: The South African Library, Cape Times Special Collection and AFRAPIX. Special thanks are due to Dave Hartman for the cover photograph and for his assistance in selecting the photographs on the destruction of the squatter camps during 1986.

Abbreviations

ANC   African National Congress
BAAB   Bantu Administration Board
CAYCO Cape Youth Congress
CLPP   Coloured Labour Preference Policy
LRC   Legal Resources Centre
NUSAS National Union Of South African Students
PFP   Progressive Federal Party
SAP   South African Police
SADF   South African Defence Force
UDF   United Democratic Front
UF   Urban Foundation
UWCO United Women's Congress
UWO   United Women's Organisation
WCCA Western Cape Civic Association
WCDB Western Cape Development Board
WPCC Western Province Council of Churches

Chronology

1986

January

1 Hundreds of activists from UDF-affiliates flee 'fathers' in New Crossroads. Nomzamo creche in KTC burnt, as well as the house of Sybil Dwangu of UWO.

2 Four people reported dead following conflict in New Crossroads. Winnie Nkosi and two other women reported to be held as hostages in an empty container in Old Crossroads.

3 Prince Gobingca tells reporters that the revenge attacks of the 'fathers' are because of the disrespect of the youth and hand grenade attacks on homes in New Crossroads.

4 First arrests for 'Kangaroo courts' in the Cape Peninsula.

6 Bodies of two men, buried in the Guguletu cemetery, removed.

7 Chris Heunis blames youths for all seven 'murders' in KTC and New Crossroads between Christmas Eve and January 4. Sam Ndima releases Winnie Nkosi and others from Old Crossroads and warns 'comrades' that the residents of his community will not tolerate petrol bombs and 'Kangaroo courts'. 4th reported 'necklace' victim in the Cape Peninsula since November, 1985.

9 Positions for community guards advertised in edition of WCDB's publication.

11 Reports of 200-300 'witdoeke' from Site C in Khayelitsha attacking residents in Nyanga East and KTC.

13 WPCC tries to mediate between comrades and 'fathers' or 'witdoeke'.

14 Hundreds of women and children flee KTC, fearing a further attack by 'witdoeke'.

16 KTC men and comrades patrol KTC until satisfied that threat of attack from 'witdoeke' has passed.

21 At WPCC peace talks, 'fathers' apologise for assaults.
24 UDF officially calls of the consumer boycott.
28 Four reported dead in renewed outbreaks of violence at KTC.

February

3 P.W. Botha announces that influx control will be scrapped by 1 July, 1986.
6 Institute of Race Relations reports that 714 people have died since July, 1985 — an average of 3,2 people per day.
7 WCDB announces that no more people will be arrested for pass offences in the Western Cape.
20 Massive security swoop in Guguletu.
22 800 women in rent protest in Khayelitsha.

March

3 Seven suspected ANC 'terrorists' gunned down in broad daylight in Guguletu.
17 ANC flags fly at funeral for those killed in Guguletu shoot-out. 30 000 attend and defy magisterial ban against political content at the funeral.
20 House of a man suspected of attacking two young women whose families are questioning the 'bail fund' in New Crossroads is burnt down.
21 Two New Crossroads' Committee members killed by comrades from the community.
22 Seven die, two houses burnt down in conflict between New Crossroads' residents and 'witdoeke' from Old Crossroads.
23 New Crossroads' Committee members visit the *Cape Times* and allege that the 'organisations' have been trying to remove them from the area for years.
25 Two policemen killed in separate incidents in Nyanga Bush and the Portland Cement squatter camp. Two youths ambushed and killed by security forces hours along Lansdowne Road, after the deaths of two policemen.
26 Nkosana Mdini, a 'witdoek' hostage from Old Crossroads, tells reporters that two Casspirs escorted the 'witdoeke' into New Crossroads. UWO, CAYCO, and the WCCA issue a statement condemning the actions of Ngxobongwana and the police.
28 Troops patrol the townships.

31 Melford Yamile (Nyanga Bush) and ten other arrested under Section 29 of the Internal Security Act.

April

1 300 women protest against Ngxobongwana at No. 2 School in New Crossroads.
5 100 women protest at Caledon Square in Cape Town against the detention of Yamile and others from Nyanga Bush. Leading Old Crossroads' residents call on 'progressive organisations' to help them oust Ngxobongwana from the area.
13 Sam Ndima calls a meeting at Noxolo, Old Crossroads, and says that he has been given guns by the police in Athlone.
17 14 people, including 5 from UDF-affiliates, appear on charges of murder for the deaths of 9 people in New Crossroads.
19 Pass laws officially scrapped.
22 Three die in renewed fighting between youths and 'witdoeke' in Nyanga Bush, near the WCDB offices.
24 Sam Ndima, Prince Gobingca and others from Old Crossroads visit Col. Schreuder of Athlone police station to ask for guns to 'protect' them from the comrades.
29 Site C meeting addressed by Sam Ndima who threatens the squatter leaders from Nyanga Bush, Nyanga Extension and Portland Cement. Petrol bombings, stonings, and burnings reported along Lansdowne Road. Elliot Dyakophu, former Old Crossroads' Executive member, has stones thrown at his house. Christopher Toise's house attacked at 3 am by security forces. Albert Naphakade's house in Old Crossroads demolished.
30 Delivery vehicle gutted in Guguletu.

May

1 Crossroads' complex sealed off by security forces. Police and Sam Ndima visit Dyakophu's house searching for arms. Sam Ndima addresses meeting in Old Crossroads and says he has been given 200 guns by the police.
2 Le Grange announces that funeral curbs will be enforced.
5 Hand grenade thrown at Ngxobongwana's house.
6 SACLA clinic closed down by Executive Committee in Old Crossroads.
7 Former Executive Committee members and residents known to be

critical of Ngxobongwana flee Old Crossroads.

16 Residents of the satellite squatter camps hear gunshots in the area.

17 Attack on Portland Cement squatter camp begins at midnight.

18 9 am — Further attacks on Portland Cement and houses burnt. 10 am — Toise's house is burnt down by 'witdoeke' accompanied by two white policemen. 11 am-4 pm — residents run from burning Portland Cement to Nyanga Bush and along Lansdowne Road. More attacks on Portland Cement. Nyanga Bush, then Nyanga Extension attacked. 4 pm-5 pm — residents along Lansdowne Road attacked. 10 pm — 'witdoeke' leave the devastated areas.

19 Remaining shacks at Portland Cement burnt down. Destruction continues until 9 am Tuesday morning. Massive relief operation begins for over 20-30 000 refugees.

20 Refugees at Zolani Centre, Nyanga, intimidated by security forces and told to go to Khayelitsha. Protest meeting held in Cape Town by a variety of church and service organisations.

21 Barbed wire erected along Mahobe Drive.

22 Continuing outcry and condemnation of the attack on the squatter camps and calls for a judicial enquiry. Chris Heunis affirms that homeless refugees are to move to Khayelitsha and the upgrade of Old Crossroads to continue. Timo Bezuidenhoud relieved of his regular duties to concentrate on the upgrade project.

23 Raids on KTC by the security forces and fears that a further attack is imminent. KTC leaders and former leaders of satellite camps prepare to bring a court interdict against the security forces and 'witdoeke' restraining them from unlawfully entering KTC.

25 UDF holds protest meeting in Mitchells Plain.

30 Urban Foundation pulls out of Crossroads' upgrade scheme.

31 Security forces raid the home of Sophie Benge in New Crossroads. 2 500 refugees move into Khayelitsha. 350 squatters move into shacks at Mpetha Square and Lansdowne Road. Alfred Siphika appears on charges of attempted murder of a 'witdoek'.

June

4 Rebuilding of shacks continues in Nyanga.

6 Chris Heunis rejects the possibility of the refugees living anywhere other than at Site C.

8 Rumours of an attack on KTC.

9 8 am — 'witdoeke' gather at the Administration Board offices.

10 am — Zolani Centre is attacked. 11 am — 'Witdoeke' enter KTC, burning houses and looting, while security forces stand by. 11.30 am — Police fire at returning residents. 1 pm — 'Witdoeke' enter KTC again and attack houses. 3.30 pm — Police prevent KTC residents from entering camp to retrieve their belongings. 4 pm — 'Witdoeke' withdraw.

10 9 am — 'Witdoeke' gather. 11.30 am — Comrades gather along ridge at KTC. 12 pm — 'Witdoeke' enter KTC and then retreat. 1.15 pm — 1 000 KTC residents advance down NY5 to Nyanga Extension to create defence barrier. Women from KTC plead at parliament. 3-5 pm — Repeated confrontations between 'witdoeke' and comrades. Relief operation collapses.

11 KTC and Nyanga the scene of continuing unrest. Three journalists hurt, one fatally — George De'ath.

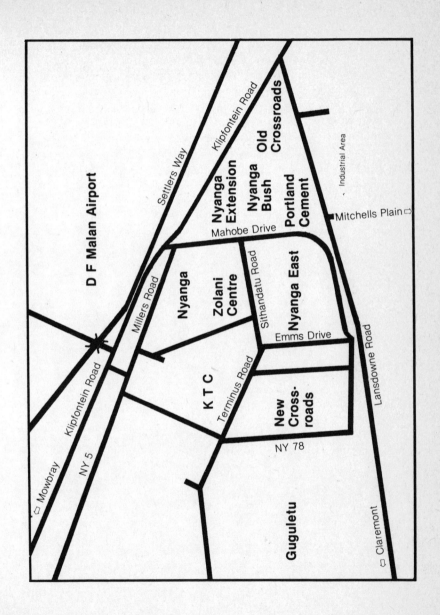

Introduction

During May and June of 1986, the local and international public witnessed one of the most brutal forced removals of squatter communities ever to take place in South Africa. In two separate but related paramilitary operations, residents from Old Crossroads, wearing bits of white cloth to identify themselves — hence the name 'witdoeke' — forcibly removed over 70 000 people from the surrounding squatter communities. In less than a month, the 'witdoeke', with the uncontested support of members of the SAP and SADF, had removed not only the most consistently resistant squatters in the Cape Peninsula but, also, and perhaps more crucially, the support bases for UDF-affiliated organisations operating in the area. During this process, squatter linkages with progressive organisations were severed and, for the moment, political control returned to local state authorities — black and white. In a series of bold strokes Crossroads, once a symbol of defiance and resistance to the removal strategies of the apartheid state, had become a symbol of right-wing vigilante reaction or 'black-on-black' violence. The long-held dream of local political activists of incorporating Crossroads into the progressive movement had turned into a nightmare.

To make sense of contemporary conflict, and the shifting political alliances which have accompanied it, one requires some understanding of past and present social dynamics within squatter communities such as Crossroads. It is important to realise, for example, that the ongoing 'witdoeke' versus 'comrades' conflict did not arise out of a vacuum. It should be understood as the culmination of a long and complicated political process taking place within squatter communities in the Cape Peninsula. Why, one asks, did Crossroads, a former symbol of defiance to apartheid strategies, align itself with elements of the South African state and participate in the forced removal of adjacent squatter communities? The answer to this question — so crucial to any broad understanding of recent events — must be sought through an analysis of the community's complex history.

Perhaps no other South African squatter community is as well known as Crossroads. Its eleven-year history, which corresponds with the political and economic crisis of the South African state, is not easily captured or understood. Much of the literature to date has tended to concentrate on struggles taking place between squatters and the state. Less has been said — until the more recent developments made it impossible to ignore this dynamic — about social stratification within squatter communities themselves. Yet, as this study begins to reveal, it is precisely because of social divisions that opportunities have been provided to local and central state authorities, as well as to social actors within these communities, to effect strategies of divide and rule — and, eventually, to destroy a community.

A central argument of the following book is that the political economy of Crossroads has been shaped and transformed by the simultaneous strategies of internal leaders and representatives of the local and central state. No analysis of broader squatter politics in the Western Cape can afford to ignore the significance of the social forces which, over time, helped to influence the direction and orientation of the Crossroads leadership. An underlying theme concerns the various forms of social agency which impinge upon, and help shape the ideology and political orientation of these communities, as well as the nature of their ideology and political practice. Although this book begins to tackle some of these issues, and raises others which I am as yet unable to address, further work and research is needed to do justice to the complexity of the struggles and issues which I identify.

This book, based in part on post-graduate research,[1] was in the making long before I embarked on formal academic study at the University of Cape Town. A number of years working directly in Crossroads as a community worker, as well as ongoing observations and analysis of events taking place in Crossroads and other squatter communities, provided me with opportunities, and initiated the desire to develop a deeper understanding of the community as a whole. The growth of divisions, the escalation of violence, and the increasing levels of repression within Crossroads forced me to abandon fieldwork in the community at the beginning of 1984. These events became a catalyst to a critical reflection on the nature of the community's leadership and political practice. As repression and violence persisted, I became more and more convinced that coming to terms with the history and dynamics of a squatter community like Crossroads could perhaps lead one to identify broader social processes.

Leaving Crossroads provided me with an opportunity to pursue some of the historical and theoretical issues which I had begun to question while working in the community. It soon became evident that any analysis of Crossroads as a community, or the political choices of its leadership, had to consider the broader political and economic forces which had shaped and influenced its direction over time. The way in which broader state strategies were in turn shaped by some of the struggles taking place within Crossroads, and the surrounding squatter communities, also needed to be taken into account. It is this dialectical process which I try to capture in the following book.

The book should be read, then, as a first attempt to develop a much deeper understanding and analysis of Crossroads. It is essentially my own personal attempt to give back to the residents of this and other squatter communities of the Cape Peninsula something of the history they made. In the face of tremendous pressures from the South African state and from within their respective communities, they found the courage and will to resist oppression: had it been otherwise, this study would not have been possible.

Sources

What one can achieve in terms of reconstructing the past is to a large extent determined by the extent and character of surviving sources. This study has utilised a variety of sources but has largely relied upon the participant observation of the author and interviews conducted with the residents of Crossroads and the surrounding squatter communities between 1980 and 1986. Although a substantial amount of documentation exists, particularly in the form of newspaper reports, these fail to capture how the people of Crossroads experienced and understood their social environment at specific moments in time. The use of oral history, with its in-built limitations of bias and subjectivity, nonetheless remains an invaluable method in recreating the histories of black communities in this region.

As a participant observer I was often able to verify evidence supplied by oral informants. I was also in a position to document events as they took place and acquire knowledge and insights about issues, meetings and struggles which might otherwise have been lost to history. The reader should, however, be alerted to the fact that as a participant in many of these events, my view of them has been informed by my own experience and political perceptions.

Writing a book which describes a contemporary phase of history has meant that I have had to confront the fact that many of the people and organisations identified and described remain active in their various spheres of influence. Certain political choices have had to be made. However much I may have agonised over the wisdom of writing a history which, by its very nature, raises controversial political issues, it was not written with the intention of levelling accusations. What I have attempted to do is to try and reveal something of what Eugene Genovese calls 'the complexity, contradiction and tragedy that [defines] all human experience'.[2] I have done so in the hope that all of us may learn valuable lessons in the process of making history.

Historical Background

Before looking at the history of Crossroads and other squatter communities which emerged in the course of the 1970s and into the 1980s, it is necessary to locate these developments within a much longer tradition of community formation and destruction. This tradition threw up new forms of struggle and resistance to the trajectory of capitalist development in the country as a whole. In the Western Cape, where a regional history of working class struggles has as yet to be formulated, little is known of the social tragedies which must have accompanied capitalist development. What is known at a more generalised level, however, is how state policy changed towards urban Africans in the decades between 1900 and 1970. This was the period when social and political control over the African population visibly intensified.

Only a century before the emergence of Crossroads, the majority of the African population in southern Africa lived in independent chiefdoms.[3] The mineral discoveries of the late nineteenth century, and the industrial revolution which accompanied them, profoundly transformed the lives of all of South Africa's inhabitants. As the country became more and more linked to international capitalist networks, new strategies of labour control developed.

The migrant labour system which evolved dictated who could live in the urban centres and how, once there, their lives would be regulated. Migrants' struggles, their daily experiences, and the forms of consciousness which developed in the urban areas, remained intricately linked to the nature of the labour system which underpinned their lives. This labour system, premised as it was on a process of incomplete proletarianisation, continued to reinforce cultural and material linkages to the rural areas. This has had profound effects upon the formation of the South African working class and, as a result, remains fundamental to any study of class formation or forms of working class consciousness in this region. As an issue raised in the course of my own work, but not adequately developed, it remains a crucial area for further research and analysis.

Economic growth in the Cape was closely linked to mining developments on the East and West Rand. As the construction industry boomed, especially around the docks, an increasing number of migrants entered the city. By 1900 an estimated 10 000 Africans lived in greater Cape Town. Most of them were concentrated in overcrowded tenements and lodging houses.[4] As early as 1901, the first forced removal of a 'black spot' took place in the city. According to a recent study, armed soldiers and trucks moved hundreds of Africans from the city centre to a newly built location on the outskirts of Cape Town, called Uitvlugt.[5] Within less than a decade the majority of the inhabitants of this location — now renamed Ndabeni — were either back in the inner city, or squatting on the periphery in West London (Athlone), Ysterplaat and Maitland.[6] It was only through an intensive campaign of raiding and harassment that the local municipality found itself, by 1916, able to increase Ndabeni's population to 1600 residents. The vast majority of the city's African population then, as now, inhabited informal settlements beyond the immediate control of the local authority. Many of those who squatted did so to escape local controls; others because housing failed to keep pace with the level of economic development or labour needs. In Cape Town, as elsewhere in the country at the time, little of the capital accumulated was re-invested in public housing projects.[7]

Residential segregation and the principle that 'Natives' were only permitted into municipal areas for labour purposes were formalised in the Urban Areas Act of 1923.[8] This coincided with the Cape Town City Council's demands that the central government should enforce stricter controls over urban Africans.[9] When the Act was applied in Cape Town in 1926, only 12% of the African work force employed in private industry registered. In an attempt to escape the noose of tightening controls, the vast majority of Cape Town's African work-force avoided registration and residence in prescribed locations. A census taken of the inhabitants of Langa (built in 1927), showed that only a small percentage of the city's African workforce was living there. As has been the case historically in the Cape Peninsula, most chose to inhabit squatter settlements on the edges of the city.[10]

None of the existing legislation to limit urban African settlement was effectively applied in a period of escalating economic growth. The Urban Areas Act of 1945 — intended as it was to check the flow of Africans to the cities — was implemented only half-heartedly in the context of continuing post-war industrial expansion. In Cape Town, for example, the urban African population increased at a rate of 9,8% p.a. between 1936 and 1946.[11] By 1948, the local squatter population was estimated to be in the region of 150 000. Within months of the Nationalist Party's election, there were strong indications that those in power were intent on implementing existing legislation to control the location and allocation of African workers in the urban areas.

As early as August 1948, the Minister of Native Affairs warned that the government was reviewing the presence of the African population in the Western Cape and deciding whether or not to reduce it drastically. The next year he confirmed that the government was intent on reducing the squatter population and that local authorities had been given the necessary power to begin doing so.[12] It was not very long before intention became reality. A series of raids in late 1948 and early 1949 resulted in the arrest of what were now considered 'illegal' Africans. An intensive onslaught against the urban African work force began when Eiselen became the new Secretary of Native Affairs in 1949, and Hendrik Verwoerd the Minister in 1950. Squatters and African women became the primary targets in effecting a policy directly concerned with the influx, efflux and reproduction of the African workforce. In the following decade, informal squatter settlements in the Cape Peninsula which housed the majority of the 'illegal' surplus population — for example, Cooke's Bush, Windermere, Vrygrond, Marabestad, and Eureka — were confronted by a state determined to gain control over every aspect of the inhabitants' lives. Little work has thus far been done to reveal the effects of this process in the Western Cape. What evidence does exist suggests that the urban African masses did not passively acquiesce in the presence of an increasingly interventionist state. The important role played by African women as primary targets of pass raids, legislation and harassment remains a significant feature of the 1950s.[13]

Eiselen, when Secretary of Native Affairs, paid particular attention to the presence of African women in the Western Cape. In a paper entitled 'The Coloured People and the Native' he noted that an increase in the settled African population could be related 'not only to the influx of new migrants but also to internal increase . . . to women following up their men and having children'.[14] He also complained about the 'illegal concentrations of Bantu the cities' and live in 'uncontrollable' squatter settlements. Along with the numerous pass raids of the early 1950s, Eiselen introduced a more indirect form of social control — 'controlled' squatter camps which he described as 'the most practical method of tackling the housing problem within a short time'.[15]

In 1954, when a deputation of women from the Blouvlei squatter camp, led by Dora Tamana and Ben Turok, met with the City Council's Manager of Native Affairs following a series of police raids on the camp, the implications of government policy for Africans in the Western Cape were spelled out in no uncertain terms:

> The policy of this government is to reduce the number of African families in the Western Cape . . . . The labour needs of the Peninsula are to be met by migratory labour . . . . The government intends to have one central location for families at Nyanga therefore the people of Windermere, Blouvlei and other squatter camps will be moved there en masse. Those who have the right to stay will be allowed to remain, the rest will go home . . . . [16]

By May 1956, at least 5 000 of the Peninsula's African population, many of whom had been living in 'black spots', had been resettled in the newly established Nyanga Emergency Camp. Thousands of African women were endorsed out of Cape Town. The memory of this major resettlement and removal process, which gave rise to incredible personal hardship, remains deeply embedded in the consciousness of an older generation within Cape Town's African population.

The economic boom and political quiescence of the 1960s was predicated on a number of factors. These included the smashing of extra-parliamentary opposition and trade union activity; low wages; a favourable comparative advantage in world markets; and increased foreign investment. As the economy boomed, with manufacturing output increasing at an unprecedented rate of 8,4 per cent p.a., it produced a number of significant features. A great deal of concentration and centralization of capital took place, especially in the manufacturing, wholesale and retail, construction and transport sectors. The technology employed in this process led to the increasing marginalisation of the work-force as a whole. In spite of the high growth rate of the decade, structural unemployment remained a critical feature of the South African social formation. Attempts to maintain and increase control over the urban African work-force took specific forms in different regions of the country. In the Western Cape the form of labour control and allocation became known as the Coloured Labour Preference Policy (CLPP).[17]   The CLPP had profound effects on the lives of Africans in the Western Cape, especially women. According to Noel Robb, a veteran of the Athlone Advice Office, women were not allowed into the Western Cape for the purposes of seeking work from as early as 1961. Many women who had registered with the local labour bureau when passes were issued in the early 1950s were immediately endorsed out of the area when they became unemployed. Many who had been here since the 1930s failed to qualify for urban rights because they were told by local officials to start counting fifteen years from the time they were first registered:

> If African women hadn't already done fifteen years since they'd registered in 1954 or 1955, they were immediately endorsed out when they became unemployed . . . . Most, even though they had been here since 1934 or 1938 had to start counting fifteen years from the time they were registered . . . many could not prove their case and so they were endorsed out.[18]

Women who were de facto heads of households, and therefore economically active, suffered a differential form of economic and gender exploitation. Instead of endorsing them out of the area, officials offered them six-month temporary permits, provided they left their children in the rural areas. This was known as the 'bread-winners clause'.

> It was the most immoral thing because they had to choose between dumping their children in the Transkei or working. The choice was really between working or going back with the children and starving. All just about chose to stay and work. Many of them have been on six-monthly permits ever since.[19]

By 1967, Cape Town's legal African female population had decreased from 18 639 (1951) to 15 716. By corollary, the city's illegal population was on the increase. The full implications of the CLPP would only become visible in the decades to follow — especially its effects upon African women. In the survival struggles of the 1960s, against a state which intervened at every level of their lives and against men who seemingly colluded in this process, some women began to develop a consciousness of their differential oppression. How women responded to this oppression in the course of their day-to-day lived experiences remains an essential feature of class struggle in South Africa as a whole. It is also crucial to any understanding of the important role African women played in the formation and defence of squatter communities in the Cape Peninsula.

Restrictive labour policies which aimed at reducing the size of the urban African work-force were only effectively applied in times of less demand from capital. From 1968 to 1974, the needs of local capital in the Western Cape led to a reversal of earlier trends. The number of contract workers, for example, increased by 56,3% during this period despite legislative restrictions.[20] Profit margins were kept high by keeping the social wage of the urban work-force low. As a result the housing shortage for the Peninsula's black population had reached critical levels by the early 1970s. By 1974, a large number of informal squatter settlements dotted the Peninsula's social horizon. Many of those who inhabited these camps were migrants and women who, in one way or another, had managed to survive in the interstices of the urban areas rather than return to the desolation of the homelands.

When the economic recession set in the state once again began an onslaught on the working class in its cities. Against a backdrop of economic pressures and the growing political threat of the urban black masses — signalled by the Durban strikes of the early 1970s — the South African state moved against the surplus population in its cities. Squatter settlements which housed a significant percentage of this population became the primary targets of state repression. However, when the state moved against these settlements it found itself challenged by organised resistance in the Western Cape for the first time since the 1960s. Reducing the size of the reserve army of labour and especially relocating women back to the homelands proved a far from easy task. Crossroads, whose early inhabitants had their roots in the bitter survival struggles of the 1960s, soon emerged at the forefront of resistance to removal.

Notes

1. See J. Cole, 'Crossroads 1975-1985: From Community to Mini-Bantustan', BA Hons Thesis (UCT 1986).
2. E. Genovese, 'On Being a Socialist Historian', *In Red and Black* (London 1971), p.10.
3. S. Marks and R. Rathbone (eds.), *Industrialisation and Social Change in South Africa* (London 1982), p.1.
4. See C. Saunders, 'Not Newcomers', *South African Outlook* (Cape Town 1978), for more details on the early history of Cape Town's migrant workers.
5. See B. Kinkead-Weekes, 'Africans in Cape Town: The Origins and Development of State Policy and Popular Resistance to 1936', MA Thesis (Cape Town 1985).
6. Ibid., p.85.
7. See E. Koch, 'Without Visible Means of Subsistence: Slumyard Culture in Johannesburg 1918-1940', B. Bozzoli (ed.), *Town and Countryside in the Transvaal* (Johannesburg 1983).
8. This policy was first formulated by the Stallard Commission of 1921.
9. See I. Goldin, 'The Poverty of Coloured Labour Preference: Economics and Ideology in the Western Cape', *SALDRU Working Paper*, No.59 (Cape Town 1984), p.6.
10. See M. Budow, 'Urban Squatting in Greater Cape Town, 1939-1948', BA Hons Thesis (UCT 1976), for details and statistics on early squatter settlements and locations in Cape Town at this time.
11. C. Simkins, *Four Essays on the Past, Present and Possible Futures of the Distribution of the Black Population of South Africa* (Cape Town 1983), p.39.
12. *Cape Times*, 21.8.1948 and 19.4.1949.
13. The Prevention of Illegal Squatting Act, Native Laws Amendment Act and Abolition of Passes (and Co-ordination of Documents) Act were key bits of legislation aimed specifically at illegal squatters and African women. See J. Schreiner, 'Thina Singoomama Asina Kubululwa: Forms of Organisation by the Federation of South African Women in the Western Cape', BA Hons Thesis (UCT 1982), and J. Cole, 'When Your Life is Bitter You Do Something', D. Kaplan (ed.) *South African Research Papers* (Cape Town 1986), both of which attempt to document the early struggles of African women in the Western Cape against the implementation of this represssive legislation.
14. W. Eiselen, 'The Coloured People and the Native', *Journal of Racial Affairs* (1955) 6,3, p.7.
15. Ibid.
16. S.A. Rogers, quoted in J. Cole, *op. cit.*, p.25.
17. First introduced in principle by Eiselen in the mid-1950s, the policy had a number of aims which included: reducing the size of the African population; a 'freeze' on the construction of family housing; and an attempt to make it extremely difficult for African women to obtain urban residential and employment rights. After 1968, contract workers could no longer qualify for permanent rights, nor could they bring their families to the cities legally. The CLPP was implemented through a number of amendments to the Black Labour Regulations and Urban Areas Act of 1945.
18. N. Robb, Interview (Cape Town 1984).
19. Ibid.
20. See I. Goldin, *op. cit.*, for a detailed analysis of the reversal of the CLPP.

Chapter 1

Crossroads — The Early Years

In February 1975, a number of people began moving onto a piece of land bounded by Lansdowne Road, Mahobe Drive and Klipfontein Road, east of Nyanga township in the Cape Peninsula. They had been instructed to move there by officials of the Divisional Council who administered the land in the area, and by local inspectors of the newly established Bantu Administration Board (BAAB).[1] Many of the original settlers came from a nearby squatter camp known as Brown's Farm, where 'coloured' and African squatters had lived together for years.

> One night we heard somebody arranging a meeting for all the blacks. Usually there were no meetings at Brown's Farm . . . . We were told at the meeting that during the day white men had come to say that all blacks must move. We asked 'But where to?' We were told they had said 'to the Crossroads' . . . . After two days they came back to give us notices . . . . Then they took us . . . . My aim was not to go but it was a force for us to go. They told us we would live nicely there just like at Brown's Farm. Unfortunately when we came there it was just a bush. A lot of trees and just a few houses . . . . There were less than fifteen families there. It was really a shock to us. On the other hand we did have a hope because we thought if our husbands were qualified, they would give us houses and rights to stay. But unfortunately it didn't happen as we thought.[2]

Setting up a 'transit camp' for African families at Crossroads was part of a more generalised weeding-out process taking place in the Cape Peninsula in the course of the early 1970s. Resettling people temporarily at Crossroads was seen as the first phase of reducing the size of the surplus African population. Local BAAB officials would soon find, however, that Crossroads residents saw this as a permanent, not a temporary solution to their housing needs.

The Early Residents

Who were the early residents and where did they come from? According to a study in the late 1970s, most of the original settlers had lived in Cape Town for over ten years. During this time an estimated 30% had lived in an average of two to three other squatter settlements. A significant percentage had lived in the surrounding black townships prior to moving to Crossroads. Of the male population, 50% were employed, either as contract workers or permanent workers in the Peninsula. Only 9,3% of the women in the community had legal rights to be in Cape Town.[3] By the middle of April 1975, through a process of authorised resettlement and gradual illegal occupation of the land, over 7000 Africans were reported to be living in the area, in an estimated 1027 shacks.[4]

In the course of these first few months, migrants, petty traders, women, the aged, youth, the unemployed, the employed and the unemployable all found a home in Crossroads. Here they would jostle side by side in their common struggle to survive the harsh realities of the apartheid state. As time went on residents from all backgrounds and class positions would begin to forge a popular alliance against removal. The process began shortly after the first eviction notices were handed out to the residents in March, 1975.

Organisation and Resistance

In Crossroads, community organisation and resistance grew in response to changing local circumstances. The first eviction notices were ignored. The initial sanctioning of the settlement by local BAAB officials gave the people who moved into the area a sense that their occupation of the land was legitimate. This widely held belief had been given material substance by the fact that local officials had not only instructed people to move to the land, but had helped them set up a rudimentary infrastructure on their arrival. Mrs Ndamase, one of the first residents of Crossroads, was even told that she could expect services such as water taps, refuse and rubbish removal.[5] This strongly held belief in the legal and moral right to occupy the land, coupled with years of removals in the Cape Peninsula, soon proved a formidable obstacle to local officials' plans for further removals.

After a series of raids on the area in March, residents realised that the officials were determined to remove them from the land. Mass meetings were held in 'open fields' to discuss the matter. These were not by any means spontaneous. They were organised by rudimentary committee structures in the community, consisting of a Men's Committee, initially under the leadership of a Mr Nyembezi, and an ad hoc Women's Committee, led by Jane Yanta and Elizabeth Lutango. These two women were elected at a community meeting to contact outside organisations like the Black Sash to assist the residents in their struggle against the evictions. Johnson Mdayi, a member of the Men's Committee, was asked by the men to accompany the women. According to a Committee member present at the time, he was asked to 'act as a link between the community, the lawyers, and the Athlone Advice Office'.[6] The residents of Crossroads contributed to this process by donating 20 cents each at community meetings. Although the men and women worked together during this period, it was the women who first made contact with outside individuals and groups. One of the first recorded meetings between the women of Crossroads — a delegation of thirty women — and the Athlone Advice Office took place as early as March 1975. The Advice Office was one of the few organisations in the Peninsula concerned with the issue of rights for the urban African population. Many of the women of Crossroads would probably have visited this office in the course of the 1960s and early 1970s for help with pass offences and other related issues. Their cases would have been dealt with on an individual basis. But in 1975, for the first time in the history of the Advice office, women without legal rights sought collective action. Noel Robb remembers that a group of 'determined' Crossroads women arrived 'unexpectedly' at the office that day, asking for assistance. There were a number of factors about the meeting that she recalls as being highly significant.

In early 1975, for the first time we had women coming to us . . . . Now in the first place we didn't even know what Crossroads was . . . and the one thing we noticed was that these women were very independent . . . . When we told them that they were illegally in the area, they told us that in spite of that they were determined to stay. There was no question that they would obey the law. Now

that was the first time that we had heard of that. Until 1975 when
you did everything you could to get permission for a woman to
stay, and you failed, she went. But the women of Crossroads were
the first women to sit in our office and say... "We are not
going".[7]

The vanguardist role women played in the early struggles of
Crossroads is a significant feature of its history. This is not surprising
given the hardships many African women experienced in the Western
Cape, particularly after the Nationalist Party came to power. Many of
the women who took part in the visit to the Advice Office had either
been forced into an illegal existence in the city's black townships during
the bitter years of the 1960s, or had struggled to survive alone with their
children in the desolate homelands whilst their husbands worked in the
cities. It was these experiences which helped inform their actions and
consciousness during the 1970s. Many women who settled in
Crossroads were prepared to make public what for them had previously
been an individual experience of personal pain. Their sense of oppression, by the apartheid state and by their husbands, is captured in the
following account. The speaker is a woman from Crossroads who later
became a community leader.

We lodged in Guguletu but it was really terrible. When you are a
lodger you are not free . . . . You just pay rent . . . . We were
two families there . . . and the inspectors were arresting me a lot.
I did have rights to be in Cape Town, but when I got married I
went to the office and they gave me 'phuma phele' [endorsement
out of the city] because my husband was not qualified to be here.
He didn't have 10 years at his job. My husband didn't like the
arrests all the time and he pleaded with me to go to the Transkei
where his mother was living. I didn't want to go but life was
getting too difficult on this side. So I went . . . . I took my littlest
children with me . . . . We went to Ncamaqa. You take a bus
from Idutywa to get there. And it was a desert. No bushes, no
trees, just flat land. It was terrible, really terrible to me. No
factories, no shops, nothing . . . . I had to go miles to find a doctor . . . . I lost both my children, one from bronchitis the other
from measles. For two years it was such a hard life for me. I don't
know how I did carry it out. Sometimes we were starving . . . .
There were days when I didn't even have money for matches . . . .

But I had to stay. Every time I wrote a letter to my husband, but he never wrote back. I decided, alright I will show him. I had a Singer machine so I sold it for trainfare . . . . I came back to Cape Town unexpectedly. He had a shock when he saw me. And I found that when I came he was a playboy . . . staying with girlfriends . . . . I was so sick and thin. I decided then that I will never move anymore.[8]

Frustration and the beginnings of a proto-feminist consciousness are clearly evident in this woman's account of her life during the 1960s and early 1970s. It was this hidden strength and spirit of resistance which would become public and visible in the context of the struggle to remain in Crossroads. As women began to share with each other some of the pain of these individual experiences, they began to develop a sense of solidarity as women. Many began to identify their frustration in terms of national and sexual oppression. The migrant labour system had over the decades intensified gender conflict, resulting in the bitterness and frustration which this woman clearly expressed. The entry of Crossroads women into the public sphere of politics must be understood as directly related to their experiences of life and struggle.

The solidarity of the women of Crossroads was reinforced by the presence of the Women's Committee which acted very much as a mutual-aid society during these years of early resistance. The many pass raids which accompanied the eviction notices in 1975 directly affected women in the community. Those arrested were assisted with bail money and the paying of fines with funds collected at community meetings. The Women's Committee played a major role in raising these funds.

The raids of 1975 were part of a generalised onslaught against illegal Africans in the Peninsula. As the economic recession intensified, so did the pass raids. In the course of the year over 23 000 influx control cases were heard at the Langa courts — an average of 105 per day.[9] Little could be done to stop the raids. Their overall effect, however, was to strengthen social cohesion. The consistent presence of an external threat was fundamental in creating solidarity and unity amongst the residents of Crossroads. It also assisted in the transformation of the hitherto 'provisional' settlement into a more organised and structured community. Both the Men's and Women's Committees were instrumental in this process. But it was the determination of the women that inspired much of the community's resistance.

Community Consolidation

> Men [and women] make their own history, but they do not make
> it just as they please, they do not make it under circumstances
> chosen by themselves, but under [those] directly encountered,
> given and transmitted from the past.[10]

In the years between 1976 and 1978, when Crossroads faced its next
major threat of removal, significant changes took place. As the
residents responded creatively to their social environment, new community structures were created, old ones were transformed, and distinctive patterns of leadership emerged. The growth of community cohesion
was underscored by income-generating possibilities — for example, a
burgeoning informal sector developed after 1976.[11] In the struggle to
survive, residents from different social backgrounds began to share a
common Crossroads culture.

The consolidation of any community can only become a material
reality if it is left relatively undisturbed for a period of time. The
objective conditions for Crossroads to consolidate its infrastructure and
unique identity became possible in 1976 when the Cape Town Divisional Council tried to utilise a recent Amendment to the Prevention of
Illegal Squatting Act to remove residents from the land they had
occupied for over a year. The Council submitted an application to the
Supreme Court in Cape Town to have Crossroads demolished on the
grounds that it constituted a health hazard. They argued that the
services provided were inadequate for the entire population, then
estimated at 10 000 people.[12]

Mike Richman, who in the course of later struggles would become the
official Crossroads lawyer, and Rev. David Russell, an Anglican priest
working in the area, assisted residents to oppose the application.
Mdayi, who had become chairman of one of two Men's Committees
when the initial committee split into two in early 1976, became the
opposing applicant in the court case. In his affidavit Mdayi applied for
Crossroads to be declared a legal Emergency Camp, in terms of Section
6 of the above Act. The Supreme Court ruled in favour of the Mdayi
application, largely due to contradictory evidence led by the BAAB and
Divisional Council, neither of which wanted to take ultimate responsibilty for the demolition of the camp.[13] As a result, Crossroads was
declared an Emergency Camp in June, 1976, and the Divisional Council
was instructed by the courts to provide rudimentary services such as

water taps, refuse and night soil removal for a nominal service levy — R10 per month.

When the Crossroads community celebrated their first major legal victory, they did so in isolation from other social upheavals taking place in Cape Town and the rest of the country. For June 1976 was the time of the Soweto uprisings which, as Colin Bundy recently reminded us, 'rippled from their eponymous centre into 200 communities around the country'.[14] These major events seemed far removed from the inward-looking and particularist concerns of the residents and leadership of Crossroads. The full implications of this national event would only affect the community at a much later date. For the moment local residents turned their attention to consolidating control over their social environment. The legal victory of 1976 gave them the chance to do so.

Situated on land administered by the Divisional Council, and therefore not by the local BAAB, Crossroads enjoyed a unique position as a black community in the Cape Peninsula. Unlike other black townships, it was not subject to the constraints which operated in these areas — for example, lodger permits, trading licences and strict political control. As a result, the area became something of a 'liberated zone'. In Crossroads opportunities existed for the implementation of alternative economic and political initiatives. The creation of structures to ensure effective control over their own environment became a concern of the leadership from as early as 1976. Whereas much of the community infrastructure had operated on an ad hoc basis in 1975, after the legal victory of 1976 it started to become more formalised. In the residents' attempts to improve their community, they were supported and encouraged by a variety of outside individuals and organisations — for example, the Black Sash, the Quakers and the Institute of Race Relations. Relationships with these liberal organisations had been established in the course of the legal battles of 1975 and 1976. Their assistance was not only welcomed but actively sought. In Crossroads, unlike other black communities in Cape Town in the late 1970s, whites were welcomed. This firmly established relationship with liberal institutions became a strong influencing factor on the consciousness of the residents, particularly the leadership. For a long time to come, this consistent exposure to bourgeois ideology would predispose the leadership to trust the judgement of their liberal friends and to be wary of more radical political interventions. Political alliances with individuals and groups other than white liberals were not actively pursued by the leadership. A concern to conserve the relative freedom they had won in the course of these early struggles, supported by liberal friends, would make the leaders and residents of the community vulnerable to future reformist initiatives.

The construction of two local schools during the years 1976-1977 assisted in building a sense of permanence and community spirit. Both the Sizamile and Noxolo schools were built with the direct participation of local residents. School committees were elected to supervise day to day administration. Teachers were from the community and initially paid by funds collected from the residents. Noxolo and Sizamile became symbols of the determination of the people of Crossroads not only to stay on the land but also to improve their social environment:

> We had a lot of children and we didn't want them to be just running up and down . . . so we collected money and old clothes to sell . . . . The children and the parents also had to help . . . . Each child had to bring zincs, nails, and poles, and in this way we put together the school . . . . At that time everyone was proud to help because people could see we were in need and that we must do something to get something . . . .[15]

The two schools soon became meeting places for the local committees — two of which adopted the names of the schools. The original Men's Committee had split into two by 1976. It appears that the division had arisen over a dispute relating to funds collected for lawyers. After the Black Sash offered legal assistance, there was no longer a need for community funds to be raised. Mdayi, a member of the Men's Committee, reported this development, but a number of men were unhappy about returning funds already collected. As a result the Committee split. Mr Mdayi took one half with him, whilst the other half went with a Mr Selani. Mr Vicki, chairman of the Men's Committee at the time, resigned. Although there were now two committees they did not operate as opposing groups. They co-operated in the growing task of administering the area. The only marked difference between the two was that Sizamile had women members whereas Noxolo had only men.[16]

As the population grew after 1976, committee members felt the need to zone the community and extend the network of local authority beyond the committee structure. Two informal bodies were established at this time — the homeguards and wardsmen. The homeguards acted as a type of community police, concerning themselves with resolving petty crime in the area. Wardsmen, on the other hand, had the function of settling local disputes and collecting funds for specific community needs. Wardsmen were elected by residents of the four major sections or wards in Crossroads. Both Sizamile and Noxolo had wardsmen and homeguards attached to them. The two committees, together with these two informal bodies, functioned as a local authority in the community.

Membership often overlapped. One could serve as a committee member as well as a homeguard or wardsman. As a result, information and decision-making did not become the monopoly of any one community structure. According to residents living in Crossroads at the time, report-back meetings were regularly held, ensuring that members remained accountable to a broader constituency. The committees and other structures were perceived as functional to social control, and do not appear to have been established for coercive or exploitative purposes. Although corruption may have occurred on a small scale, it is not something that residents identify as characteristic of the period.

In Crossroads there was room to create alternative forms of local control. Why these early residents chose these particular forms is something which requires explanation. In the context of a new environment, social groups draw on previous experiences and cultural assumptions. It is not surprising that the structures which evolved in this new setting were influenced by what Koch calls 'the cumulative result of struggles and activities of previous generations and periods'.[17] In relative terms most of the residents of Crossroads were recent arrivals to the urban areas. One can assume that their material and ideological linkages with the rural areas had not been completely severed: a total rupture with former social processes and ways of understanding their world had not necessarily taken place. The forms of social control established in Crossroads and the consciousness of many of its residents were infused with old notions and beliefs. In the struggle to adapt to a rapidly changing social environment, the people of Crossroads chose familiar structures. Male-dominated and modelled as they were on the 'invented tradition' of bantustan structures, they were not necessarily intended to, nor did they in fact, completely replicate their functions. Once in place, however, these neo-traditional structures served to reinforce and perpetuate material and ideological linkages with the rural areas. No resident at the time could have anticipated the full implications of this train of events. It was this headmen-and-wardsmen system that would one day be used to further the exploitative objectives of the state and certain individuals in the community. This will be explored later.[18]

The Women

During this period the women in Crossroads concerned themselves less
with forms of local authority than the men and concentrated on specific
issues which affected them. Although it was possible for them to be
members of the Sizamile Committee, most chose to work instead as
part of the Women's Committee. In 1976, Regina Ntongana became
chairwoman, replacing Jane Yanta. Under her leadership, the women
developed into a formidable force in the community. The specific role
of the Women's Committee in the history of Crossroads would eventually become a site of struggle. As the women began involving
themselves in issues which some of the more conservative men considered their sphere, gender conflict began to surface:

> Between 1975 and 1977 we came to be strong as women. We used
> to have meetings every day, sharing our views and thoughts on
> each and everything . . . . We decided we must have a few in
> front to lead so that we must be definitely sure who is going to
> work. So we elected thirteen women, I was one of them. At first
> the men didn't like it. They said we did things too fast . . . it
> wasn't easy for the men because they were working during the
> day . . . the women was going all over the place to find out what
> was going on . . . . So we knew more than the men . . . . Some of
> them were really jealous . . . they sometimes stopped us to have
> meetings.[19]

The Women's Committee, unlike that of the men which tended to
have membership along fairly strict geographical lines, drew members
from all sections of the community. During this early period the women
tended to concentrate on educational issues, developing links with outside liberal organisations, some of whom, with their assistance, ran projects in the community.[20] As time went on these women, either
unemployed or employed in the informal sector and therefore more in
touch with day to day problems, slowly developed into a much more
powerful force within Crossroads than either of the Men's Committees.
When the community once again found itself faced with the threat of
removal in 1978, it was not surprising that it was the women of
Crossroads who took the lead in the resistance.

State Offensive — Community Resistance

The relative security of the residents of Crossroads began to shatter in 1977 when the state moved against other African squatter settlements in the Cape Peninsula, many of which had sprung up at the same time as the Crossroads community — for example, Modderdam, Unibel, and Werkgenot. In the course of a country-wide attempt to remove potential urban flashpoints after the Soweto 'uprisings', these squatter settlements were amongst the first to receive the South African state's attention. Unlike Crossroads, they enjoyed no legal status. As a result, they were much more vulnerable to repressive strategies.[21]

In February 1977 Marais Steyn, the Minister of Community Development, announced that all illegal squatter settlements in the Bellville South area would eventually be demolished. In spite of limited community resistance, a series of legal battles and relatively widespread public support, all three squatter camps had been brutally destroyed by the beginning of 1978. Their destruction revealed the South African state's determination to remove the Peninsula's surplus population.

Crossroads was not unaffected by these events. In the course of the demolitions, many of the inhabitants of these squatter camps sought refuge in the community. According to the annual report of the Divisional Council (1978), the population of the community jumped from 16 900 in June 1977 to an estimated 20 000 in December.[22] Numerous raids took place at this time in an attempt to flush out the refugees. Local BAAB inspectors also tried to get committee members to 'police' the area for them. This they refused to do.[23] Within weeks of Unibel's destruction in January 1978, Dr Vosloo, Deputy Minister of Plural Relations, announced that 'Crossroads would be treated in exactly the same way as Unibel'.[24] The South African state soon found this to be a difficult task.

From the beginning, because of Crossroads' legal status as an Emergency Camp, the state was forced to use indirect tactics to remove the residents. In the course of the 1978 offensive against the community, a number of such tactics were utilised. These included: threatening to demolish the houses of residents with rent arrears; frequently serving residents with eviction and demolition notices; articles in the liberal and Afrikaans press trying to discredit the community's image as law-abiding and crime-free; the harassment and arrest of women collecting water at taps on the edge of the community; and when all of these failed, a series of 'crime-prevention' raids in September in which hundreds of residents were arrested.

The immediate effect of these 'motivational' efforts was to galvanise organisation and resistance. This occurred at two levels — inside Crossroads and amongst individuals and organisations with long-standing links with the community. Within weeks of Vosloo's announcement, the two strands of resistance coalesced into what became known as the 'Save Crossroads' campaign. Those who participated soon became locked into an ideological battle with the state:

> Crossroads gradually became the best publicised squatter camp in
> the world. This was not by chance: it was the result of a
> deliberately and intelligently designed awareness campaign. The
> people of the camp and those in sympathy with them realised that
> a continuing blaze of publicity was the best protection against
> demolition and other harassment.[25]

In Crossroads, organised resistance to removal was led from the beginning by the Women's Committee. With the assistance of two community workers from a local church organisation, the women began to restructure their Committee to facilitate better organisation and mobilisation of the women in the community.[26] For the first time they elected a secretary and treasurer. Office bearers were elected at one of the mass meetings held every Wednesday afternoon at the Noxolo community hall. At the same time branch committees were formed in the four major sections of the community. These branches, each with its own set of office bearers, were ultimately accountable to the central executive of the Women's Committee. For each of the state's offensives against Crossroads the women laid on a counter-offensive.

For example, when the Divisional Council threatened to demolish the homes of residents in arrears with rent, the Women's Committee established a rental sub-committee to assist local residents with loans from funds raised through the South African Council of Churches.[27] State propaganda depicting Crossroads as a slum was countered by the formation of work-teams of women, organised by the Committee. These women painted houses and generally embarked on a 'clean up' of the area. The Committee ensured that this was well publicised in the press. Although most of the resistance was essentially reactive, it did nonetheless foster a sense of solidarity amongst women in the community.

In addition to this, a new structure emerged inside Crossroads — the

Joint Committee. It was made up of the Sizamile, Noxolo and Women's Committees. This was the body which called mass meetings to report on and discuss developments taking place. The Joint Committee called mass meetings as often as three times a week, as well as over weekends, during this period. Although all three committees participated on the Joint Committee, the women soon emerged as the dominant grouping, given the fact that they attended most of the support meetings outside, and because their consistent presence on a day to day basis provided them with much better information on developments taking place in the community as a whole. The leadership role of the women was not something which the men readily accepted. There were often occasions when conflict between men and women surfaced. But on the whole gender conflict was subsumed by the overall threat of removal. In 1978, the increasingly political role of the women was, to say the least, tolerated.

The outside support group which spearheaded the 'Save Crossroads' campaign became involved as early as February 1978. During the year they held twice-weekly meetings. A 'Tuesday' group met at the offices of Mike Richman, by now the official Crossroads lawyer. Organisations represented in this group included the Black Sash, Urban Problems Research Unit (UPRU), VERITAS, the Institute of Race Relations, the Quakers, and a variety of other church bodies. A few members from the Crossroads Women's Committee regularly attended these meetings.[28] Strategies decided upon by the 'Tuesday' group were usually executed by another group which met weekly in a church hall in Claremont. They will be referred to as the 'Friday' group.

The 'Friday' group consisted of a broader range of individuals from many of the organisations and bodies represented at the Tuesday meetings. Most members of the 'Tuesday' group attended both meetings. The energy expended by this group was vast, and is best revealed by a brief summary of some of the initiatives they undertook in the course of a six-month campaign. These included: 'Stand Up for Crossroads' bumper stickers; Crossroads postcards; photo exhibitions, for example at the Baxter theatre; slide-shows; newspaper inserts and feature articles; information briefings with embassy officials and overseas journalists; organising visits to Crossroads for visiting VIPs, for example Rev. Jesse Jackson; a week of solidarity at the University of Cape Town, organised by NUSAS; a petition to save Crossroads, organised by the PFP, which managed to collect at least 35 000 signatures in the space of six weeks; and a Day of Prayer and Solidarity, celebrated not only in Crossroads but in cities and churches throughout the world.[29]

Despite this intensive resistance campaign, the South African state moved directly against the residents of Crossroads in September 1978. In two major 'crime-prevention' raids over 900 people were arrested. In the raid of 14 September scores were injured as residents fought back against riot police and BAAB officials. At the end of this major raid, Crossroads had its first martyr — Sindile Ndlela — killed by a riot policeman in the early hours of the morning. The raids were condemned at local and international levels. Local capital, represented by the Urban Foundation (UF) — a body set up after the Soweto riots of 1976 to promote a stable urban black middle class — perceived the state's action against Crossroads as a major threat to economic and political stability. In the latter half of 1978, especially in the aftermath of these raids, monopoly capital began to take an increasing interest in finding solutions to the escalating conflict in Crossroads. After the September events, the role of the UF became much more directly interventionist.[30]

Monopoly Capital, the State, and Crossroads

By the late 1970s it was becoming increasingly clear, especially to the business sector, that the Nationalist Party under Vorster could not provide the political and economic restructuring necessary to move South Africa beyond the 'crisis' it found itself in after the Soweto uprisings. The death in detention of Steve Biko, the squatter demolitions in the Cape Peninsula, together with intensified pass raids, bannings and detentions, had the effect of deepening the 'crisis' and ultimately leading to an alliance between monopoly capital, the military and individuals representative of these two power groups in the Nationalist Party. It was this new historical bloc which eventually rose to power in the wake of the 'Information Scandal' of late 1978. Crossroads immediately found itself caught in the political dynamics which accompanied the shift in the balance of national political power.[31] In the course of September and November 1978, at least two known meetings took place between representatives of the UF and a few members of both the Sizamile and Noxolo Committees. The Women's Committee was totally unaware of these meetings, arranged with the assistance of the black male community workers from VERITAS. According to 'confidential' minutes of the September meeting, the UF informed committee members that 'the business community of South Africa, and particularly the UF, were extremely concerned about the Crossroads situation'. The UF told the committee members that they had been making representations to the government *on their behalf* 'for a considerable period'. Committee members when asked what they wanted the UF to do, encouraged them to continue their initiatives. As one resident said, 'it was better to climb a ladder rung by rung rather than climb two rungs and then attempt to climb five at once and then fall'.[32]

At a follow-up meeting in November, attended by the chairmen of the Sizamile and Noxolo Committees — Elliot Waka and Johnson Ngxobongwana — as well as the Director of the UF, Judge Steyn, the UF informed committee members that at the request of Connie Mulder, Minister of Plural Relations, they had once again submitted a proposal *on behalf of Crossroads*. In it the UF proposed that the government build 3000 houses at a cost of 15-18 million rands, on the condition that 'the government gave some land tenure to blacks' and 'relaxed' the 1968 Black Labour Regulations. In other words, the UF was asking for the scrapping of the CLPP.[33] Monopoly capital was desperately searching for alternative solutions to deal with thorny influx control issues such as Crossroads. The meetings were indicative of their ongoing attempt to maintain the conditions necessary for capital accumulation. But the kind of reformist stategies the UF were seeking could not be provided by 'verkrampte' Afrikaners like Connie Mulder. It was only when P.W. Botha became Prime Minister, in late 1978, that monopoly capital found the man to spearhead such initiatives. When Dr Piet Koornhof took over the portfolio of Minister of Plural Relations from Connie Mulder, the UF had finally found their man.

Notes

1. The mechanism for carrying out this resettlement was the Bantu Administration Board. Twenty-two such bodies had been established nationally between 1971 and 1972 in terms of the Black Affairs Administration Act of 1971. These local authorities were set up to take over the responsibility for black affairs previously in the hands of the 'white' local authorities.
2. J. Cole, *op. cit.*, p.15.
3. See J. Cornell and J. Maree 'Sample Survey of Squatters in Crossroads, December 1977',*SALDRU Working Paper* No. 17 (Cape Town 1978) for a wide range of statistics on the early residents of Crossroads.
4. See D. Russell, *Crossroads Squatter Camp* (Cape Town 1975), for residents'

accounts of these early years and invaluable statistics.

5. Ibid.
6. New Crossroads Resident, Interview No.1 (1986).
7. N. Robb, Interview (Cape Town 1984).
8. See Chapter Two of J. Cole, op.cit., for a longer account of this woman's life history.
9. G. Ellis, 'Africans in the Western Cape: A Chronology', *SALDRU Working Paper*, No. 50 (Cape Town 1983).
10. K. Marx, quoted in S. Hall and T. Jefferson, *Resistance through Rituals* (Birmingham 1977), p.11.
11. See D. Dewar and V. Watson, 'Urbanisation, Unemployment and Petty Commodity Production and Trading: Comparative Cases in Cape Town', D.M. Smith (ed.), *Living Under Apartheid* (London 1981).
12. The 1976 Amendment to the Prevention of Illegal Squatting Act introduced a penalty of R500 and/or 12 months' imprisonment for owners or lessees of land occupied by illegal squatters. Squatters were no longer in the legal position to contest demolition of their shacks. For details on the Supreme Court application brought by the Divisional Council, see NUSAS, *We Will Not Move* (Cape Town 1978).
13. In an earlier court case, Mrs Peter of the Women's Committee had overturned a conviction for 'illegal trespassing' on appeal, precisely because of a dispute between BAAB and the Divisional Council over who had responsibility for the administration of the land.
14. See C. Bundy, 'South Africa on the Switchback', *New Society* (London 1986).
15. J. Cole, op. cit., p.17.
16. New Crossroads, Interview No.1 (1986).
17. E. Koch, 'Doornfontein and its African Working Class, 1914-1935', MA Thesis (Witwatersrand 1983), p.13.
18. See E. Hobsbawm, 'Introduction: Invented Traditions', in *The Invention of Tradition* (Cambridge 1984) for an interpretation of the concept 'invented tradition'. For Hobsbawm it is taken to mean 'a set of practices, normally governed by overtly or tacitly accepted rules and ritual of a symbolic nature, which seek to inculcate certain values and norms of behaviour by repetition, which automatically implies continuity with the past'.
19. J. Cole, op. cit., p.16.
20. For example, the Quakers ran literacy projects at Noxolo school and the Women's Movement for Peace ran sewing projects.
21. See A. Silk, *A Shanty Town in South Africa* (Johannesburg 1981) for a detailed study of the formation and subsequent destruction of one of these squatter settlements — Modderdam.
22. *Cape Times*, 21.1.1978.
23. New Crossroads, Interview No.1 (1986).
24. *Cape Times*, 22.2.1978.
25. Quoted from K. Kiewet and K. Weichel, *Inside Crossroads* (Cape Town 1981), p.51.
26. VERITAS was a sub-committee of the Western Province Council of Churches with the broad objectives of community development. Celeste Santos and the author were the two community workers who participated in the re-organisation process.
27. The SACC donated R20 000 to the rental sub-committee for this purpose. The funds were channelled through the WPCC and administered by the VERITAS community workers and members of the sub-committee.
28. The women who regularly attended were Mrs Ntongana, Mrs Yanta and Mrs

Lutango, veterans of the Women's Committee in Crossroads.
29. Simultaneous church services and solidarity meetings were held in England, Holland, Germany, Canada and the United States on July 30, 1978.
30. For statistics and more detail on the September raids, see NUSAS, *We Will Not Move* (Cape Town 1978).
31. See D. O'Meara, 'Muldergate and the Politics of Afrikaner Nationalism', *Work in Progress*, 22 (Johannesburg 1982).
32. Minutes of a meeting between the UF and representatives from the Noxolo and Sizamile Committees, 28.9.1978.
33. Minutes of a meeting between the UF and representatives of the Sizamile and Noxolo committees on 6.11.1978.

Chapter 2

The Politics of Reform and Co-operation

> A crisis occurs, sometimes lasting for decades. This exceptional duration means that uncurable structural contradictions have revealed themselves . . . and that, despite this, the political forces which are struggling to conserve and defend the existing structure itself are making efforts to cure them within certain limits, and to overcome them. These incessant and persistent efforts . . . form the terrain of the conjunctural and it is upon this terrain that the forces of opposition organize.[1]

The restructuring or reform of any society, as Gramsci argues, tends to take place 'within certain limits'. It eventually leads to a new 'settlement' which, as Stuart Hall notes, does not just 'emerge' — it has to be *constructed*. Political and ideological strategies are required to 'disarticulate old formations and rework their elements into new configurations'.[2] From late 1978, the South African state, personified by Piet Koornhof, attempted to find solutions to the Crossroads struggle — '*within certain limits*'. Few were prepared for the political implications of Koornhof's reformist intervention. The process he set in motion within days of taking office as the new Minister of Plural Relations profoundly transformed the nature of the Crossroads struggle.

'Piet Promises' in Crossroads

> We stayed like that struggling until Dr. Koornhof came in 1978. Before he came the authorities were definitely sure that they were going to demolish Crossroads. They said it was filthy dirty and used lots of other things as excuses to try and demolish Crossroads. When Koornhof came he stopped Crossroads from being demolished.[3]

On Koornhof's first day as new Minister of Plural Relations he learnt of a right-wing plan of the SADF, SAP, Railway Police and local BAAB officials to destroy Crossroads. The idea was to surround the camp and remove the illegal residents in buses and trucks to trains which would presumably have taken them back to the homelands. The plan was 'leaked' to a member of the Crossroads support group who, in turn, contacted the press. When the *Cape Times* phoned Koornhof to ask for a comment, he immediately sprang into action, turning a potentially disastrous moment into a bold political stroke of genius. Koornhof made it known to the press and Mike Richman that he intended to come to Cape Town and talk directly to the people of Crossroads. As far as he was concerned no 'bloody bulldozers' would be used against the community on his first day in office. He went on to promise a new era for urban blacks.

> The department is a link between white and black. We want to create an atmosphere of friendliness and goodwill . . . . One of the most important parts this government has to play is . . . how the so-called urban black will fit into the new constitutional plan . . . .[4]

In late November, on his first full day in office, a smiling Piet Koornhof visited Crossroads and addressed residents at the Noxolo community hall, especially decorated for the occasion. Koornhof made it clear that he 'did not want to raise expectations'. It was evident from the responses of committee members that local residents did indeed have expectations. When Tyson Tom, a Noxolo Committee member, conveyed this optimism to Koornhof he immediately responded. Koornhof's reply is revealing not only of his general attitude towards black people but also of the kind of solution he had in mind for the Crossroads community.

> A good father will always be careful not to arouse expectations which cannot be fulfilled, but he must also bear in mind the best interests of his *children* at heart. I will try my level best, with my officials, to act in the best interests of the people of Crossroads. But the best interests are sometimes not what one wants immediately — one must understand that. *I do not think this is the best place for you to have meaningful lives.*[5]

Koornhof's visit signalled a new historical phase for Crossroads. In the months and years ahead, his divide and rule strategies would transform the nature of squatter struggles in the Cape Peninsula. Crossroads was the first urban black squatter community to become the target of these reformist strategies. After Koornhof, Crossroads would never be the same.

The 'Negotiations'

Let there be no misunderstanding. There is a policy and there is a law. That is why your co-operation is so important. With your co-operation it may be possible to find a solution to the problem . . . . I will do everything possible to look at Crossroads as a problem in itself.[6]

In December 1978, one month after Koornhof met the residents of Crossroads, a proposal was submitted to him, at his request. It was drafted by Mike Richman, the Crossroads lawyer, on the instructions of the Joint Committee. The proposal contained two suggested solutions to what Koornhof called the 'Crossroads problem'. Firstly, the Joint Committee proposed that Crossroads should remain at its present location and be 'transformed . . . into something quite new'. This proposal, which the Committee referred to as 'the most desirable' was in essence a proposal to upgrade basic services and housing at Crossroads. The second option, which the Joint Committee considered 'less desirable', asked for 'permanent accommodation . . . of the whole community in some place in Cape Town, other than on the existing site'.[7] The submission of these proposals was a preamble to a process of negotiations which Koornhof had indicated would take place in early 1979. As soon as they began in January, it was clear that Koornhof had decided upon a solution long before the 'consultations' began. For him, as he stated at the initial meeting, 'Crossroads was a place . . . [leading] to some other place'.[8] The Crossroads leadership would find themselves unable to negotiate their first demand — upgrade of the community on its present site.

Koornhof's solution was spelt out at a second meeting between himself and a delegation elected to represent Crossroads demands. This meeting, like the one before it in January, took place in the H. F. Verwoerd building in Cape Town. The delegation consisted of seven representatives from the Joint Committee (five men, including a 'youth', and two women); two community workers from VERITAS; Bishop Patrick Matolengwe of the Anglican Church; Mike Richman; and Francis Wilson, a professor of Economics at UCT. All had a long-standing relationship with the Crossroads community.[9] The 'Crossroads delegation' soon found itself caught up in a long and difficult political process.

Koornhof proposed building 'a proper Crossroads with the blessings of Almighty God'. This new township would be built on land 'adjacent to Nyanga'. He also indicated at the February meeting that he had recently solicited the support of local business organisations.[10] Francis Wilson, on hearing Koornhof's own proposal, which was in effect the second and 'less desirable' proposal of the Joint Committee, expressed what he believed to be the feeling of the delegation — 'I think that our first reaction was one of slight breathlessness'.[11] Koornhof's response to Wilson is indicative of his political style — 'Just absolutely correct and just keep it up'.[12] Koornhof, apparently confident that he had the upper hand, tried to bulldoze the delegation into accepting his solution then and there.

Wilson tried his best to redirect the discussion back to the first option of an upgrade scheme on the present site. But Koornhof, obviously irritated, responded somewhat facetiously, 'What is an upgrade scheme?' As far as Koornhof was concerned, Wilson had been put in his place and the matter closed. Tyson Tom, a Noxolo delegate, tried to support Wilson in his request that the discussion return to the upgrade proposal. He made it clear to Koornhof that no agreements could be made before the delegates from Crossroads held a report-back meeting with the community as a whole.

> I think what we are after is to get more information or we shall not be able to report to anyone . . . . We may find that we bring back a bottle without saying what is inside . . . . Lastly, if you can bear with me, I wonder as to whether Dr. Wilson was through with what he was saying . . . .[13]

Koornhof, unable to do otherwise, allowed Wilson to put forward the case for the Crossroads delegation. Wilson proceeded to argue that no settlement could be agreed upon which would divide the community. He made it clear that the delegates from the Joint Committee had received no mandate from the community to engage in any agreements that might in any way result in divisions. It appears that he did not attempt to try to convince Koornhof of the feasibilty of an upgrade scheme. Instead he asked for more details on the proposed new township. Koornhof replied that 2575 sites were envisaged and that he could *in no way* give concrete assurances that the houses would only be for Crossroads residents. He also asked the delegation to keep the contents of the discussion confidential. This the delegation and their 'advisers' appear to have accepted unquestioningly, since no discussion on this issue is reflected in the minutes of the meeting.[14]

At least one other known meeting took place between Koornhof and the Crossroads delegation at the H. F. Verwoerd building. This occurred in March. When local reporters asked the delegates from Crossroads to comment on the negotiation process, they refused, saying that 'the Minister had asked them not to divulge details . . . to the press'.[15] Throughout the months of 'negotiations' only a handful of people — inside and outside Crossroads — had full knowledge of what was taking place. The Crossroads support group, for example, which up until the end of 1978 had met at least twice a week to share information, had disintegrated into a variety of small caucus groups. The most powerful of these, in terms of access to information and the leverage to intervene directly in the process, was the informal group which revolved around Mike Richman and Francis Wilson. Caught up in the dynamics of negotiating with Koornhof, they had little sense of accountability to the broader support group. They shared information and strategies only when pressurised to do so by a small minority who were feeling increasingly peripheral to the discussions taking place.Whenever this group raised critical questions they felt they were treated as something of a 'lunatic fringe'.

The difficulty they faced is clearly demonstrated by the outcome of one of the few occasions when this minority was able to persuade Richman and Wilson to convene a special support group meeting to review what was taking place. Most, but not all, of the 'Tuesday group' were present. At the meeting, Wilson and Richman presented their draft of a blueprint which suggested various categories under which Crossroads residents would qualify for the proposed new township. There was dissatisfaction amongst a number of people present over the apparent acceptance of government categories in this proposal.[16] The fact that these same categories reappeared in the final Koornhof statement on Crossroads in April, *almost word for word*, reflected the minimal power most support group members had to influence the direction or pace of the negotiations. The future of

Crossroads appeared to lie in the hands of a select few.

Those who remained consistently critical of the direction and pace of the negotiations, as well as the content of the 'reforms' being offered by Koornhof, found themselves increasingly marginalised and, on some occasions, were even labelled 'radicals'. Kim Weichel, a researcher for the Urban Problems Research Unit (UPRU) at the time, and Keith Kiewet, a local journalist, reflected the general attitude of the support group towards what was considered to be a radical position, and therefore not to be taken seriously, in a book they co-authored on Crossroads in 1980:

> The confusion about the proposals was fanned by some white community workers who rejected a compromise solution on the grounds of ideology. Some of them were enjoying confrontation politics and appeared to lose interest once the compromise had been reached.[17]

Inside Crossroads itself, a fair amount of confusion existed as to whether or not to trust Koornhof. To do so meant to go against most people's prior experiences when dealing with government officials; not to do so implied challenging the advice of the Joint Committee's most trusted friends. Although the delegates were open to trusting Koornhof, they drew the line at the local BAAB officials. Koornhof made it clear, however, that as far as he was concerned no solution was possible *unless* the Crossroads leaders co-operated with his local officials. This he tried to convince them to do.

> I am a preacher's son. I don't want to preach to you but you must bear with me. I believe it is in your interest to do so . . . . I have said from the beginning if you assist the officials . . . we can solve the problem in a humane way. You have heard me say often that I want *co-operation* between the officials and you. If there is *co-operation* then things go well. I have been in this department for thirty years and these officials have put up with a lot of difficulties which you don't know of and I really request that you make it easy as possible for them by *co-operating*. If I was preaching my message would be plain and simple. It would consist of two words, '*please co-operate*'. You will not be sorry. That is the way in which this problem will be solved. I wish you God's blessings.[18]

By the end of March the leaders' fears led to a breakdown in the negotiation process. They consistently feared that Crossroads would be divided and that not everyone would qualify to move to the new township. Richman and Wilson, at this point reluctant to carry on in the face of a deadlock, called in representatives from the Urban Foundation with whom they had been meeting to discuss Crossroads from time to time. This marked the beginning of the UF's more visible and active role in the negotiation process. At a meeting held at Noxolo school in early April, Judge Steyn, the director of the UF, summarised the Minister's position, and presented his own interpretation.

> . . . [A]s we understand it . . . you as a committee have no right or authority to agree to any scheme which will not help the whole of Crossroads . . . . The Minister on the other hand, says that he would like to make provision for everyone at Crossroads *but* this is impossible. He has to draw the line somewhere and I will try to explain to you where he thinks he should draw this line . . . . [Koornhof] has given the assurance to all of us that he wants to provide for *as many as possible* on the basis of humanity and fairness. The Minister is suggesting that instead of asking you as a committee to agree to a division along certain lines he will merely tell you, after listening to you, where *he* thinks the line should be drawn. He is not going to ask you to agree to it or not agree to it. All he will ask you to do is to indicate to him that if he draws the line and if he goes ahead with plans for a new home for the *whole* of the Crossroads population, *except for those few people*, he wants to know whether the community will then co-operate with him to bring this new township into existence . . . .[19]

Steyn then suggested to the Joint Committee that if they were unable to agree with what the Minister proposed, they could 'acquiesce as distinct from agree'. At this point, the Joint Committee members, unconvinced and, not surprisingly, somewhat confused, requested a meeting with Koornhof. As Tyson Tom put it, 'that which comes from the messenger is not as sure as that which is conveyed personally . . . .'[20]

Within five hours of this request, Koornhof met the Joint Committee *in Crossroads*. There was no doubt that he wanted the issue settled as quickly as possible. Ngxobongwana, chairman of the Noxolo Committee, tried to make it clear to Koornhof why the Joint Committee felt it necessary to meet him personally. One of the major points of contention was that Koornhof consistently refused to give concrete assurances that everybody would qualify to live in the new township.

> We agree and accept what the Minister says but then we get a little cold feet when the Minister does not give us anything signed that says 'this is the paper you may have to go to the other place'. Without this kind of concrete assurance, we cannot stop and say that people dealing with us are speaking the truth . . . . We are asking for some guarantees . . . .[21]

Koornhof now needed to convince the Joint Committee of his sincerity, without necessarily offering the guarantees they were asking for. This he proceeded to do. He told them how, after a long struggle within his own party, he had managed to convince his colleagues 'that the way to solve this issue was to lay out a new township of 2575 stands . . . where the people of Crossroads [could] settle permanently and I hope in very happy circumstances'. Such a township, he continued, 'could go down in history as being built in the times in which we live . . . . I will build the township *but* promise that you will give your co-operation to this . . . [and if it is built] it will be because of the blessing of Almighty God and because of many prayers said'.[22]

Before leaving the meeting, Koornhof thanked Richman, Wilson, and representatives of the UF, all present at the meeting, for their kind assistance: 'I will tell the world that it is because of this co-operation that it has been possible'.[23] The Joint Committee, after four months of endless discussions, tired, desperate, and with no other alternatives being offered to them by their 'advisers', finally 'acquiesced' to Koornhof's proposal and agreed to co-operate in building the new township. What Koornhof had, by the end of the day, managed to persuade the Joint Committee to do was to agree to a resettlement of Crossroads with no guarantees that everybody in the community would in fact qualify to live there. Four days later, before the Joint Committee had even shared this decision with the broader community, Koornhof publicly announced *his* solution to the Crossroads problem.

The April 'Settlement'

Koornhof's press statement on 5 April spelled out his proposed solution to the Crossroads issue. The categories of Crossroads residents who qualified for accommodation in the new township were the following:

1) The families of Africans who qualified for permanent residence under Section 10 (1) a or b of the Urban Areas Act;
2) contract or migrant workers and their families who lived illegally at Crossroads in order to be with breadwinners;
3) the families of breadwinners not covered by a contract or full-time employment in the area but who earned a living in some legitimate way, for example, craftsmen or persons rendering an informal service in the community;
4) persons or families who by reason of being uprooted or through other circumstances deserved special consideration.

These categories would take care of most residents of Crossroads except:

1) Those convicted of a crime involving a fine of over R500 or 6 months imprisonment;
2) a vague category of Africans who would be offered jobs and homes in the 'homelands' which, according to the statement, 'concerned a substantial number of Crossroads families';
3) those classified as 'vagrants' or 'persons or families with no visible means of support'.[24]

Koornhof's statement was heavily influenced by the Riekert proposals of 1979. In it the 'insider/outsider' dichotomy was clearly expressed. Concessions were to be given only to 'certain' categories of residents. Others, who failed to qualify, could 'elect' to return to the homelands for jobs and housing. In other words only residents with jobs and housing would qualify for resettlement. The pivotal role of the private sector in assisting with the provision of housing was also reflected in the Koornhof statement.[25] In many ways Koornhof's April statement reflected the 'verligte' position on how to deal with influx control in a way that suited both the state and capital and, in the process, divided the African working class. It would be many more years, however, before the 'verligte' line would gain hegemony within the Nationalist Party.

Koornhof's intention of utilising new methods to ensure that influx control worked in the Western Cape is clearly expressed within his press statement:

I regard it as being of the utmost importance that the representatives of organized commerce and industry in the Western Cape,
with whom I have had discussions, have pledged their full support
for *both aspects* of the plan — i.e. for the immediate implementation of the new housing project . . . and also for measures
whereby blacks who are not properly housed will not be employed
on pain of having penalties for contravention by employers and
the strict application of provisions relating to influx and squatter
control . . . .[26]

In the statement Koornhof set out the terms under which the state
would deal with Crossroads in the future. The implications of his statement were vast. In real terms it meant: placing Crossroads under the
control of the BAAB for the first time in its history; granting residents
temporary permits and not passes, making it possible for them to be endorsed out at any stage by withdrawing the permits; defusing a highly
political and embarrassing issue, especially in the eyes of the international community; offering an 'ad hoc' solution to one community
and not to the millions of other 'illegal' blacks which meant dividing the
Crossroads struggle from the broader one; and, most importantly,
using a seemingly progressive move to launch a new offensive to tighten
up influx control and, in the process, suppress resistance. The
immediate effect of the statement was to create division and confusion
inside the community and amongst the support group. In general,
however, Koornhof's 'reprieve' was received positively by outsiders
who in the euphoria of the moment failed to analyse the full implications of his statement.
The liberal press, for example, welcomed the statement in toto.
Bishop Tutu, usually an outspoken critic of apartheid, hailed the
announcement as 'a wonderful step in the right direction in a country
where feelings are running high'.[27] Not one of the usual critics of apartheid appeared able to see that Koornhof's statement implied that influx
control would be tightened up by strictly applying legal provisions
relating to the pass laws and squatter control. A year later in an interview in *Die Burger*, Koornhof was even more explicit about his perceptions of how the state was forced to deal with Crossroads.

Crossroads [was] an unusual situation. Actions which are usually
valid, cannot apply here. On account of its unique nature, ad hoc
decisions had of necessity to be taken . . . . Crossroads must not

be seen in isolation. Squatting is a phenomenon which occurs all over the country, and the world . . . . The problem can only be solved if sufficient *work and accommodation* is provided *in the black states* . . . . We must strengthen our hands. People must stop complaining that too much is being done for the blacks. That which we expend in the development of the black states must be viewed as the *premiums of our insurance policy for the future.*[28]

Inside Crossroads, there were mixed reactions to the Koornhof statement. Sam Ndima, head of the Noxolo homeguards, voiced misgivings in the local press about the implicit division of Crossroads contained in the statement. A number of teachers from Noxolo School also expressed reservations, especially concerning the future role of BAAB in their community.[29] There were clear indications that, for some residents, Koornhof's statement fell far short of a community victory. Unlike 1976, when the residents won the right to have Crossroads declared an Emergency Camp, there was no sign of celebration. Residents who voiced doubts about the nature of their *victory*, were even more confused by the response of their 'advisers' — Richman and Wilson. At a meeting held at Noxolo, a day after the Koornhof statement was announced, they raised questions about the wisdom of making critical statements to the press. Richman advised members of the Joint Committee, and the community workers from VERITAS, to be 'positive':

If we provoke [Koornhof] and his officials by statements which suggest he is not carrying out his promises then we will be making it easier for the opponents of Crossroads to point out that he has taken the wrong course . . . . I think the *wise and sensible thing to do is to be positive.*[30]

It became increasingly evident to committee members inside Crossroads, and to a minority on the support group, that to challenge publicly the seemingly uncritical acceptance of Koornhof's statement meant some form of marginalisation. That did not mean that committee members did not continue to raise their fears inside the community. One member who did so, when asked to address a meeting of the youth at Noxolo community hall, was Johnson Ngxobongwana:

I, by myself, there are many things I am discontented with, according to this statement of Dr. Koornhof . . . . He says we are

going to a new place, but the new place we are going to, [well] I
am not sure [that] we are all going. In my mind I don't think all
[of us] will be going . . . . Most of the people are being confused
by the whole thing. Whether or not it is wrong they will take
it . . . . The people going to those houses will only be watchmen
. . . . [E]ventually people with rights will take them over . . . .
Paul in the Bible said, 'I have become more of a slave than a slave
should be'. So now what Koornhof is aiming to do is to make us
more slaves than we are now.[31]

Although the youth, together with some of the women, tried to
stimulate discussion on the 'deal', this was quickly squashed, particularly by members of the Crossroads delegation. The conflict within
the community remained limited and hidden. The only sustained and
well formulated public criticism of the negotiation process and the
subsequent Koornhof 'deal' came from NUSAS in the form of a document entitled *Would You Make A Deal With This Man?*[32] published,
according to the editorial, as 'a form of intervention . . . in a
process . . . known around the world as the struggle for Crossroads',
NUSAS called Koornhof's settlement 'one of the most sophisticated
government moves to date'.[33] The document was not well received by
members of the support group, who came under heavy fire for their role
in the negotiation process and seeming trust of Koornhof's promises of
'reform'.

In a later study, Auret van Heerden, NUSAS president at the time,
was highly critical of them, for what he termed the 'reformist
quagmire'. He argued that a key mistake of the Crossroads support
group was the fact that they saw the negotiations as a 'conclusion of the
struggle'.

There did exist a strategy and tactics but they were reformist to
begin with . . . there was no understanding of the relationship
between means and ends . . . . The Koornhof negotiations were
not considered a good tactical position but as a conclusion of the
struggle. Koornhof, on the other hand, scored all the tactical
points, appearing to be reasonable and open to change, defusing a
potentially explosive situation, while at the same time destroying
the unity of the community by employing divide and rule tactics.
The leadership of Crossroads, sincere and committed as they
were, did no more than function as the arm of capital's advanced

guard, the Urban Foundation.[34]

Van Heerden's study attempted to analyse Crossroads by comparing it to trade union struggles taking place elsewhere at the time, for example PEBCO in Port Elizabeth. He used these two case studies as 'examples which furnish contrasting examples of organisation in South Africa and the importance of a clear analysis, strategy and programme of transitional demands'.[35] Whilst his analysis remains important, in that it teased out the class nature of the Crossroads struggle, it nonetheless failed to take into account a number of important aspects of this specific squatter struggle. For example: the contradictory nature and complexity of working class struggles; and, more crucially, the limits within which squatter struggles such as Crossroads occur.

Van Heerden also failed to acknowledge that the only individuals or organisations objectively capable of making a direct critical intervention during this period — for example, the trade unions who were having to deal with the process of reform *at the same time* as the Crossroads leadership (1979) — placed their priorities elsewhere. Progressive support was given on the whole to struggles at the point of production rather than to those taking place in communities where the working class was being reproduced. The failure of the trade unions, and the left intelligentsia, to take squatter struggles seriously would eventually prove to be a crucial miscalculation for the continuation of working class resistance in the Western Cape.

A further point that needs to be made, however, is that any direct critical intervention in Crossroads by a more progressive grouping would have been a site of struggle in itself. Entry was in no way a given. Long-standing relationships existed between community leaders in Crossroads and liberal individuals and institutions. These relationships were tenacious because they had been forged over a number of years. As a result the leadership was much more open to trusting their judgement and advice. The Crossroads leadership wanted to believe in Koornhof's promises as much as their 'advisers'. Although contradictions existed, any individual or organisation which might have challenged the direction of this struggle would have had to overcome considerable constraints. Perhaps the most formidable was the political consciousness of the Crossroads leadership itself.

They had limited demands which could easily be co-opted by a Minister trained in the art of 'realpolitik'. The fact that the majority of the Crossroads support group believed in reform made the leadership even more susceptible to reformist strategies and solutions. The people of Crossroads did not, in the final analysis, 'make their own history . . . under circumstances chosen by themselves'.[36] As a result they found themselves caught up in a process of divide and rule. As far as the state and capital were concerned the ideological battle of reform had been won and the terrain of struggle reconstructed. For the residents of Crossroads, however, the struggle had in many ways only just begun.

Notes

1. A. Gramsci, quoted in Stuart Hall, 'Moving Right', *Socialist Review* 55 (1981).
2. S. Hall, quoted in J. Saul and S. Gelb, 'The Crisis in South Africa: Class Defense, Class Revolution' *Monthly Review*, 33, 3 (New York 1981), p.3.
3. Old Crossroads, Interview No.7 (Cape Town 1984).
4. *Cape Times*, 22.11.78.
5. Ibid.
6. Dr. Koornhof, 'Unofficial Minutes of Koornhof/Crossroads Delegation Meeting' (January, 1979).
7. 'Proposals of the Joint Crossroads Committees' (December, 1978).
8. Dr.Koornhof, op. cit.
9. The delegates from Crossroads were: Elliot Waka (Sizamile Chairman), Johnson Ngxobongwana (Noxolo Chairman), Tyson Tom (Noxolo), Duncan Ndabaninzi (Sizamile), Howard Ntloko (Masizane Youth), Jane Yanta (Women's Committee), and Regina Ntongana (Chairwoman, Women's Committee). The community workers from VERITAS, a community development sub-committee of the Western Province Council of Churches, were Wallace Mgoqi and Celeste Santos. They attended these meetings as observers. On occasion, Wallace Mgoqi would act as interpreter.
10. The organisations represented at this meeting were: Western Cape Traders Association; Cape Town Chamber of Commerce; Cape Employers Association; Cape Chamber of Industries; and the Afrikaner Sakekamer of Cape Town, Parow and Bellville. According to newspaper reports, these business organisations had formed something called the 'Action Committee' in late January with the expressed purpose of finding 'a solution to the Crossroads Emergency Camp'.
11. 'Unofficial Minutes of Koornhof/Crossroads Delegation Meeting' (February 1979).
12. Ibid.
13. Ibid.
14. Ibid.
15. *Argus*, 22.3.79.
16. The author (a community worker for VERITAS), Laurine Platzky (a representative for the Anglican Board of Social Responsibility at the time), and Celeste Santos (also a VERITAS community worker), were the members of the support group who voiced the most direct criticism during this period.
17. K. Kiewet and K. Weichel, *Inside Crossroads* (Cape Town 1980), p.67.
18. Dr. Koornhof, quoted from 'Unofficial Minutes of Koornhof/Crossroads Delegation Meeting' (Cape Town, March 1979).
19. 'Unofficial Minutes, Joint Committee and the Urban Foundation Meeting

(Crossroads, 1 April 1979).
20. Ibid.
21. 'Unofficial Minutes of a Meeting between Koornhof and the Joint Committee' (Crossroads, 1 April 1979).
22. Ibid.
23. Ibid.
24. Based on *Black Sash Report on the Survey* (April, 1979).
25. The Riekert Commission, together with the Wiehahn Commission, tried to formulate an institutional and political framework through which the State could attempt the twin strategies of co-option and control over the African working class. Riekert proposed jobs and housing as criteria for urban qualification.
26. *Cape Times*, 5.4.1979.
27. *Cape Times*, 6.4.1979.
28. Translated from *Die Burger*, 20.3.1980.
29. *Argus*, 6.4.1979.
30. Transcript of author's own minutes of a meeting, Noxolo, 6.4.1979.
31. Johnson Ngxobongwana, 'Unofficial Minutes of a Meeting of Crossroads Youth' (Noxolo, 7 May 1979).
32. NUSAS, *Would You Make A Deal With This Man?* (Cape Town 1979).
33. Ibid.
34. Auret van Heerden, Unpublished Honours Thesis (UCT 1980), p.107.
35. Ibid.
36. Karl Marx, quoted in S. Hall and T. Jefferson, *Resistance Through Rituals* (Birmingham 1977), p.11.

1   *Piet Koornhof visits Crossroads (November 1978).*

2   *Local resident of New Crossroads receives the key to his new house from Administration Board Official, Mr Basson (November 1980).*

3   *Koornhof Street, New Crossroads.*

Chapter 3

Struggles for Popular and State Control

In the months and years following the Koornhof settlement, the community found itself increasingly caught up in the cross-currents of repression and reform, as well as in power struggles inside Crossroads. These included: the question of who would qualify for the new township; the nature of the township; co-operation with local state officials; and, of critical importance, which leaders would control the political economy of the community. Prior to this, struggles had largely taken place around issues like, for example, the threat of removal or, more recently, the negotiation process itself. New struggles were related to who would maintain political control over the future of the Crossroads community. They took place at two levels — above and within the community. Their outcome would result in divide and rule tactics with specific implications for the women of Crossroads — the eventual undermining of whatever political space they had previously been able to win for themselves in the community. The defeat of the women and the ascendancy to power of a new grouping of men, led by Johnson Ngxobongwana, signalled a turning point in the internal politics of Crossroads.

Ngxobongwana's Rise to Power

Although power struggles were not new in Crossroads, after April 1979 they took a qualitatively different form. As early as July, a new political alliance emerged in the community. It was as anxious as the South African state to gain control over Crossroads, and spearheading it was Johnson Ngxobongwana.

No other person has played such a crucial role in determining the historical trajectory of the Crossroads community as Ngxobongwana. Although he only gained dominance in 1979, there were indications of his political ambitions as early as 1976. One of the founding members of the first Men's Committee in Crossroads recalled the way in which he initially became part of the leadership.

> We first noticed Ngxobongwana because he used to have a small bakkie and did odd jobs for people. One thing he did was to help take the school children on outings. One day we asked him how much we should pay him for his help. But he refused. So we thought to ourselves, 'Hey, this man can be useful to us'. It was then that we elected him onto the Noxolo School Committee as a secretary and how he came to be on our Committee. He wasn't elected. We just put him there. Unlike a lot of us he didn't go to work. Even Mr Mdayi wasn't always around because he was a security guard. So Ngxobongwana was the person always around in the community. Slowly lots of things, like the reports on things happening in our absence or messages from the authorities used to get left with him. In this way Ngxobongwana got to be more and more powerful.[1]

Between 1976 and 1977, Ngxobongwana gained effective control over the Noxolo Committee, although Mdayi was the legitimate chairman. He did this through a variety of tactics. One of them was cultivating key committee members whom he believed were unquestioningly supportive of him. If any member of the committee challenged Ngxobongwana's power, he would find ways of discrediting the person, usually at a public meeting. He would then persuade Mdayi to co-opt a new member, known to be a Ngxobongwana man, onto the committee. In this way he kept the balance of power in his favour.[2]

In early 1978, a major restructuring of the Noxolo Committee appears to have taken place. Following Mdayi's decision to move to KTC in 1977, Ngxobongwana took over as chairman. A number of long-standing committee members were apparently 'chased away' by Ngxobongwana shortly after he became chairman. They had been critical of his autocratic way of running the committee. Ngxobongwana replaced these men with others loyal to him — for example, Rev. Kani and Mr Daniel. For a number of months in 1978, former Noxolo Committee members — Sakela, Ntongana, Nongwe, Mcophololo, Nontulo and Mpholombo — moved across to the Sizamile Committee, under the chairmanship of Elliot Waka. One of the few men in Crossroads who consistently stayed close to Ngxobongwana's side was Sam Ndima, head of the Noxolo homeguards.[3]

Political alliances, then as now, were fluid in Crossroads. One could be a member of Noxolo and just as easily move over and join forces with the Sizamile Committee. With the exception of a few individuals like Ndima, and of course Ngxobongwana himself, this was the way politics operated inside Crossroads. Conflict and divisions existed, but before 1979 these did not preclude the possibility of joint working relationships. Throughout the crisis period of 1978 and the negotiations, for example, the Sizamile and Noxolo committees co-operated with each other, as well as with the Women's Committee. All three were represented on the Joint Committee. Within weeks of Koornhof's April settlement things began to change.

During May, a number of caucus meetings were held to discuss the formation of a central committee in Crossroads, *under one chairman*. The meetings consisted of selected individuals from Sizamile and Noxolo, including the two chairmen — Ngxobongwana and Waka. The only outsiders present were three black community workers.[4] The Women's Committee was not represented at these meetings. The idea of having one committee and chairman to administer Crossroads does not appear to have originated with Ngxobongwana. It was Waka, from Sizamile, who introduced the notion at the first caucus meeting. According to a Noxolo member present at the time, Waka said the idea had arisen because 'some people were feeling that everything should come in one entrance'. It seems as though all those present at the meeting were in favour of centralising control. They felt it made sense because, as one Noxolo member said, 'if there is an organisation and it wants to donate something it [would have been] confusing if there [were] two chairmen'. It was also seen as 'a way to control things . . . .'[5] Up until the Koornhof intervention, it had been members of the Women's Committee who to a large extent controlled access to information, outside contacts, and any resources coming into the community. The fact that these caucus meetings purposely excluded women was a sign that centralisation meant seizing political control from them. Before this occurred, other developments took place inside Crossroads which paved the way for the election of Ngxobongwana as the community's first overall chairman.

In early June, while the caucus meetings were still taking place, the Sizamile chairman, Waka, the most highly respected leader in Crossroads at the time, suddenly died. Although no hard evidence exists to substantiate allegations, numerous residents then, and to this day, suspected that Ngxobongwana and Sam Ndima were somehow involved in his death. According to rumour, Waka was poisoned. With his death, the way was clear for Ngxobongwana to become the first chairman of the new central structure in Crossroads — the Executive Committee.

The proposed elections of one central governing body and one chairman for the entire community gave rise to growing dissatisfaction in Crossroads. Opposition came especially from members of the Women's Committee, as well as a significant number of Sizamile members. Nevertheless, elections took place in August, as scheduled. Ngxobongwana, duly elected as the Executive's first chairman, proceeded to appoint the fifteen men who made up the Executive Committee, and who were facetiously termed 'the cabinet' by the Women's Committee. Each was given a 'portfolio' — for example, education; finance; welfare and health. Oliver Memani, a former member of Sizamile, was appointed as Ngxobongwana's vice-chairman. A critical feature of the elections was that the community at large voted for the new chairman. A Crossroads resident, looking back on these elections a number of years later, saw this as a crucial mistake:

> We made a mistake when we did these elections. Our mistake was this when we nominated we only nominated fifteen men. A chairman is the man who after a committee is elected we [should] decide on. But we didn't do that. We voted Ngxobongwana in as a chief. That is how he got so powerful. If we were unhappy with anything he did, Ngxobongwana would remind us he was voted in by the residents of Crossroads, not by the Committee . . . .[6]

The Beginnings of Conflict

There were no women on the new Executive Committee. After August 1979, a form of party politics operated in the community. Bureaucratic in form and nature, the Executive began to reconstruct and transform the political economy of Crossroads to suit its own needs. One of the first things it did was to take over control of all pre-existing local committees — for example, the schools and crèche committees. Executive members with their various 'portfolios' visited these local structures, and explained to them that from now on they were expected to be accountable to, and under the direct control of, the new Executive. In some cases, especially the Sizamile School Committee and local crèches which had been operating autonomously until 1979, control was not won without considerable conflict.[7] Former Sizamile members were a constant obstacle to the Executive's ability to consolidate power.

The Sizamile Committee had been 'officially' dissolved by Waka and Ngxobongwana in July 1979, and replaced by a Working Committee whose task it was to organise and administer the elections. The Working Committee consisted of a number of 'officials' drawn from Sizamile, Noxolo, and their allied bodies (wardsmen and homeguards). The majority were from the 'Noxolo side'.[8] This was totally unacceptable to the Sizamile supporters, most of whom had been excluded from discussions about the elections. As a result, Sizamile members refused to accept the decision to 'dissolve'. They also boycotted the elections. Although they were only a small minority inside the community, their opposition was not insignificant.

The Sizamile Committee, together with its homeguards and wardsmen, continued to function, even *after* the elections. The driving force behind these 'dissidents' was a group of women who were members of both the Sizamile and Women's Committees. Feeling doubly oppressed, they openly criticised both the elections and Ngxobongwana.[9] Those who voiced their opposition were soon to find out that, after 1979, there was little room for direct criticism in Crossroads.

In November 1979 the first major confrontation took place in the community. In the ensuing conflict between the former Noxolo and Sizamile homeguards, two men were killed.[10] Violence was from then onwards firmly established as a way of dealing with internal opposition in Crossroads. After this, the hegemony of the Executive, backed by a restructured wardsmen-and-homeguard system, was relatively complete. This seemed to be the case for Ngxobongwana as well. The next threat to his hegemony, however, came from within the ranks of the Executive itself.

In the period when these power struggles were taking place inside Crossroads — May to August 1979 — the leaders had to deal simultaneously with the practical implications of the Koornhof settlement. Keeping ahead of divisive state strategies, especially on the part of Koornhof's local officials, necessitated a vigilant and cohesive leadership. Unfortunately, as we have seen, within weeks of the April settlement, divisions and conflicts were surfacing in Crossroads. Before the community became physically divided into New and Old Crossroads (1980), it found itself subject to the state's divide and rule strategies. These were already being implemented in the months before the elections, when the three committees still operated as a Joint Committee.

The Survey and the Struggle For Permits

During the negotiations with Koornhof, he made it clear that the re-settlement of the Crossroads residents to the new township was dependent on two major factors. The first was a 'socio-economic' survey to establish who would qualify to move; the second, necessary to complete the first, was close co-operation between local state officials and members of the Crossroads Committee. Both were crucial to Koornhof's more sophisticated divide and rule strategies. Although many of the leaders wanted to trust Koornhof, they were consistently fearful of local BAAB officials. As a result, events did not move quite as quickly, or as smoothly, as Koornhof hoped they would. In their attempts to deal with these two issues, the Crossroads leaders found themselves largely on their own. Richman and Wilson, for example, played a much less active role, and were mainly replaced by local representatives of the Urban Foundation. It took the UF two months of consistent struggle to convince committee members to accept Koornhof's survey. They were especially fearful of questions which they felt might divide the community, or reveal sensitive information, particularly questions which referred to residents' personal backgrounds in the homelands, or their Section 10 qualifications. The struggle over the survey revealed the confusion that had always existed in the minds of the Joint Committee members. The reality that they had 'acquiesced' in a settlement that was divisive only became clear when the 'deal' was put into practice on the ground. Tyson Tom, a Noxolo Committee member, expressed the essence of these fears at one of the many meetings held to discuss whether or not to accept the questionnaire (May-June).

> If one writes a composition you start with an introduction, then a body, then a conclusion. But already the first stage has not been straight. By the end of this composition how many will we be?[11]

As a result of these fears, Joint Committee members refused to agree to the proposed questionnaire. Koornhof, clearly agitated by the delay, phoned Richman, asking him to convey the urgency of the matter to the committee. He asked Richman to inform them that he needed their approval before leaving for overseas in late June. One of the reasons he gave for the necessity to have the survey completed as quickly as possible was that he feared his right wing might sabotage plans in his absence.[12] Richman met with the Joint Committee and tried to put forward Koornhof's 'delicate' position. But he had little success.

The Joint Committee's fears were reinforced by ongoing repression in the Cape Peninsula from which Crossroads residents were not exempt. Even while these discussions were taking place, many residents in the community were being arrested for pass offences. The tightening up of influx control, promised by Koornhof in his April settlement, was already visible. Crossroads residents were just as vulnerable as other 'illegal' blacks in the area, in spite of all of Koornhof's promises. The intensification of pass raids in the Cape Peninsula helped to fuel the leadership's mistrust of local BAAB officials and, by corollary, Koornhof. Members of the Joint Committee had never been happy with the fact that Koornhof had not given them written guarantees.

> This survey has been imposed on us [and that is why] we are justified in having fears. Dr. Koornhof never gave us guarantees, that is why we are fearful. We cannot pin him down. Recently there have [also] been roadblocks. It is no wonder we do not trust the officials.[13]

Koornhof, whose political reputation was to some degree staked on successfully resolving the Crossroads issue, was forced to make a number of concessions. On the advice of representatives of the UF, who had been meeting consistently with the Joint Committee since April, he agreed to provide residents with temporary identity documents. Koornhof also promised, via the UF representatives, that a press statement would be issued making it clear to employers that if they hired 'illegal' workers, resident in Crossroads, they would not be prosecuted. In other words, they would be exempt from the threatened fine of R500 for employing 'illegal' labour.[14] In addition to the granting of temporary permits, Koornhof also agreed to accept a modified version of the questionnaire. Questions which the Joint Committee categorically rejected — those relating to ethnicity, the homelands, and Section 10 rights — were all deleted. The Joint Committee eventually agreed to have the survey carried out. Within three days of it beginning, Frikkie Botha, the Chief Commissioner in the Western Cape, publicly stated that as far as the BAAB was concerned, Crossroads residents were not exempt from arrest. Local state officials like Frikkie Botha — a Verwoerdian bureaucrat — were openly hostile to the 'verligte' initiatives of Piet Koornhof. Botha, who had a long-standing reputation as a hardliner, made his position very clear in his press statement of 7 July:

> There is no moratorium on Crossroads arrests. Those residents who are here illegally will be arrested just like any other black person [who is here illegally] . . . .[15]

The survey, which began on 3 July 1979, was implemented by a team of forty BAAB officials — twenty white and twenty black. Twenty members of the Joint Committee were elected to accompany the officials in the field, at the request of committee members. This signalled the beginning of the 'co-operation' between local officials and the committee which Koornhof had consistently encouraged. Two weeks later, BAAB officials and representatives from the UF called an urgent meeting in Crossroads to discuss some 'worrying' preliminary results. They complained that the survey reflected an average of two families per house, making an estimated population of 40 000-50 000 people living in Crossroads. This was double the official estimate for the area. BAAB officials complained that 'bus-loads' of people had been seen 'streaming' into Crossroads since Koornhof's announcement in April. They asked committee members to 'police' the community for them. This they refused to do. As Ngxobongwana put it,

> It is not our duty to stop people coming here. There are paid inspectors to do that. All we want is to stay here. We are not interested in stopping people . . . . People are coming to Cape Town because of starvation in the rural areas, not just to enjoy the city . . . . [T]here are people in the bushes all over . . . and we are not prepared to stop them from coming.[16]

As far as is known, nothing further was ever said about this 'increase' in the size of the Crossroads population. Instead BAAB officials busied themselves with preparations to issue the six-month temporary permits 'until such time as the government makes a final decision'.[17] When Mr Pietersen from the BAAB informed committee members of the date of their issue, it immediately set off doubts and fears. Regina Ntongana, chairwoman of the Women's Committee, asked somewhat ruefully, 'Did people not realise that we would be sifted?'[18] When the 'permits' were issued two weeks later, the process of divide and rule was already well under way. Co-operation between BAAB officials and committee members, in carrying out the survey, also created the objective conditions for fraud and corruption.

Fraud and Corruption

During the period of the survey (July—August), when local BAAB officials and committee members were forced to work together closely, a small number of the officials, together with some committee members, used the opportunity to forge and sell temporary permits. This intensified after the Executive Committee took over in August. The extent of fraud and corruption became public knowledge in January 1980, when several prominent leaders in the community, including Johnson Ngxobongwana and Regina Ntongana, were arrested on charges of fraud. Police had stumbled on the case in September when two men, arrested for speeding in the Transkei, were found with a large number of Crossroads reference books in their possession. This was followed by complaints from Crossroads residents to the police that they had paid money to individual leaders for residence permits, but had not yet received them.

According to security policeman, W/O 'Spyker' van Wyk, giving evidence in 1980, as many as 80 people per day had laid charges at Caledon Square in Cape Town. He stated that 'residents with complaints' had been picked up by police at a collection point each morning 'and then returned to Crossroads later in the day'. According to Van Wyk, people had stopped coming to his office to lay complaints after a fight took place between the Sizamile and Noxolo Committees in November 1979. The name of Ngxobongwana, he said, 'had been mentioned in connection with threats and intimidation'.[19]

Local officials quickly took advantage of the situation, using the allegations of fraud and corruption to drag their feet on fulfilling the terms of the Koornhof settlement. In January 1980, when residents were to receive new twelve-month permits, many found themselves issued instead with three-month temporary permits. They had received them, local officials said, because of the 'impending investigation'. Others were encouraged to send their wives 'back' to the homelands. As a result, thousands were disqualified from residence in the new township. Timo Bezuidenhoud, who had replaced hardliner Frikkie Botha as Chief Commissioner in September 1979, publicly announced that the population of Crossroads was 'definitely not more than 23 465 people'[20] — a 100% decrease in the figure quoted by the UF and BAAB in July, 1979.

In February 1980, members of the Executive Committee, under the leadership of Oliver Memani since Ngxobongwana's arrest in January, approached Richman for legal advice on how to deal with the way local officials were trying to disqualify Crossroads residents. Richman's firm helped committee members prepare a 14-point memorandum detailing their complaints. These included: an alleged breakdown in consultations between the Executive and BAAB officials; the presence of security policemen at the BAAB offices in Nyanga, where local residents were being issued with permits; the fact that some men were being told to send their wives 'back' to the homelands; the issuing of three-month permits to lodgers when Koornhof had promised that lodgers would be given the same rights as houseowners; and the fact that the promised Appeal Committee, to hear complaints from residents disqualified from the new township, had not as yet materialised.

At a meeting in the community hall at Noxolo, attended by the Chief Commissioner and a number of his officials, Bezuidenhoud tried to sidestep most of the issues raised. He argued that as Chief Commissioner he could not comment on developments taking place in other departments — i.e. the police and security police. He tried to convince the Executive Committee members present that what was happening was not his responsibility:

> As an old magistrate I know that once a police investigation is in process it is what is known as sub judice. While a case is still hanging you cannot say anything that will get you in trouble. This is a white man's court. I don't want to say anything that will get *us* into trouble.[21]

Within days of this meeting, the security police and SAP left the Nyanga offices. This did not, however, stop BAAB officials from issuing three-month permits to some residents. Who would get houses in the new township remained an ongoing struggle in the community, as did the nature of the township itself.

New Crossroads

Throughout the second half of 1979, and well into 1980, a series of meetings were held between the Executive Committee, BAAB officials , and Mr Gerber, an official of the Department of Community Development and Planning. From the beginning of June 1979, Gerber's department had taken over the construction of the new township from the UF, despite the fact that Koornhof had promised that the UF would build the township. They proposed a rent structure of R24-R34 per month, based on family income. By the end of 1979, a deadlock had arisen between the Executive and Community Development. This was largely because residents were fearful of paying what they considered to be an unfair rent. At a mass meeting called to discuss the issue, one resident after another stood up to express his or her fears. As one of them put it, 'We find it difficult to pay R7 a month now. How can we be expected to pay such high rentals?'[22]

At a community meeting held to discuss the rent issue in November 1979, a few months before the fraud arrests, Ngxobongwana stood up and claimed to have arranged a proposed trip to a low-cost housing development in Kroonstad. The trip had in fact been organised and sponsored by the Western Province Council of Churches. At the meeting residents were asked to contribute R2000 to the R1000 'on hand'. Ngxobongwana's ability to claim responsibilty for community ventures of this kind, and make residents pay towards them, was a talent he readily exploited. It would become typical of his political practice. He used this occasion, as he would many occasions in the future, not only to bolster his own personal credibility in the eyes of the community, but also to accumulate capital. Ngxobongwana made promises almost as easily as Piet Koornhof.

> The kind of houses that *I* am going to fight for will be yours forever because you will buy them and pay R7 a month for the piece of land they will be standing on . . . .[23]

Gerber tried, on a number of occasions, to persuade the Executive that the residents of Crossroads could afford the proposed rentals. They consistently refused to agree. Gerber argued that according to the results of the survey, only 518 families would not qualify for these rentals. Eventually, Timo Bezuidenhoud was forced to phone Koornhof to try and break the deadlock. His letter to the Executive, written after the phone call, is worth quoting at some length:

> I have phoned the Honourable Minister Dr Piet Koornhof on Tuesday night (11/12/79) and explained to him the fears and

plight of the Crossroads community in regard to the proposed
housing scheme and high rentals. The Minister informed me that
nobody who cannot afford the rentals will be forced to occupy the
houses to be erected. That means that people will be allowed to
choose housing most appropriate to their incomes. Secondly, that
the planning of phase two [of New Crossroads] will be done in
conjunction and with the intimate involvement of the community.
That the houses will be within the financial ability of the persons
concerned and that a self-built scheme is not excluded . . . .[24]

Within a day of this letter reaching the Executive, the acting chairman — Ngxobongwana was away in the Ciskei — sent a letter to the
Department of Community Development. The letter stated that as far
as the Executive was concerned, there was 'no objection to the proposed
Nyanga Extension [New Crossroads] of 1662 houses being erected on
condition that a self-built scheme and/or some other form of housing
which involves the community itself, is offered as an alternative'. He
added that the Executive 'would appreciate being consulted when
details of the types of options, loan arrangements, job creation, and
technical backing [were] considered'.[25] Nine months later the first
families moved into the new township. From October 1980, Crossroads
became geographically divided into Old and New Crossroads. Their
histories would remain intricately connected, especially since
Ngxobongwana considered himself chairman of both communities. The
importance of this would only be felt at a later stage in Crossroads
history.

The Executive Splits

In the midst of ongoing struggles with the state in the course of the early
1980s, internal power struggles continued to plague the Crossroads
leadership, this time within the Executive Committee itself. The conflict
began as early as January 1980, while Ngxobongwana was in jail on
fraud charges. Oliver Memani, his vice-chairman, used Ngxobongwana's
absence from Crossroads to build up a power base of his own. One of
the original members of the Executive remembers this period as a time
of constant caucus meetings:

When Ngxobongwana was away Mr Memani tried to take control. A lot of caucus meetings were held while he was in jail.

Mr Daniel, Mr Dyakhopu, Mr Tom, Rev. Kani, and some others were involved in this. They were trying to reshuffle the Executive Committee . . . . When Ngxobongwana came out of jail [in February] he wanted a report on monies in the bank that were withdrawn in his absence. The money was gone and then the trouble started. But the Committee didn't split then. Ngxobong-wana decided to let things pass . . . .[26]

Memani was able to take advantage of a growing dissatisfaction with the way Ngxobongwana operated inside and outside of the Executive Committee. For example, some committee members accused him of having agreed with Bezuidenhoud that only 600 Crossroads residents had been left off the original survey. Memani and others argued that the number was in fact far greater. There was also a rumour that Ngxo-bongwana had secretly agreed with Bezuidenhoud that residents from KTC could move into New Crossroads. Ngxobongwana eventually backed down over the issue of the number left off the survey, later in 1981, but in the meantime he had lost considerable credibility amongst some Executive members and within the community. He had a habit of meeting with local officials without members of his Executive. This would, in the long term, prove to be a fatal weakness on his part.

Memani was much clearer in his attitude towards local BAAB officials. This was demonstrated by an incident in February 1981, when some houses in the community were demolished. He immediately issued a statement condemning the action, arguing that people were not willing to move to New Crossroads 'because they cannot afford the high rentals'.[27] Ngxobongwana, on the other hand, painted a much more positive picture of the relationship between Crossroads residents and the BAAB. When interviewed a week after this incident, he told the press that 'he was impressed by the healthy relationship between the WCAB and Crossroads residents'. He added that the WCAB was not trying to force anything on the Crossroads residents but wanted to 'build trust between white and black people'.[28] Ngxobongwana's tendency to pander to local state officials from time to time remained a constant source of tension within the Executive and amongst some residents in the community. Nobody was ever really sure where he stood.

Throughout 1981 there were a number of attempts to resolve what was becoming an open split inside the Executive. For example, at one point a twenty-four member 'Commission of Enquiry' was set up 'to

investigate matters causing strife in the community'. It consisted of
local ministers, Executive members, homeguards, and a variety of
other Crossroads officials. The commission's enquiry appears to have
been short-lived. Memani's supporters in fact later alleged that it had
been 'disbanded unilaterally by the wardsmen, clergy, peace-makers,
court Ingiwevu [local magistrates], and Executive members, with the
support of the chairman'.[29] In a desperate attempt to gain support,
Memani and eight Executive members issued the following statement
to the press:

> The call is now for the Chief Commissioner to convene a
> meeting in the interests of Crossroads to thrash out our prob-
> lems and heal the split.[30]

In the statement Memani listed two major reasons for the split: the
dictatorial attitude of Ngxobongwana, and his refusal to call or attend
Executive meetings. It was not surprising that Memani should have
called on Bezuidenhoud to 'heal' the split. Many residents and
Executive members felt that he and other local officials were fuelling
existing divisions. Bezuidenhoud, for example, was accused of
meeting with both Memani and Ngxobongwana during this time, telling each what the other said about him.[31]

The fight between Memani and Ngxobongwana was publicly played
out in the press. Ngxobongwana responded to Memani's accusations
by issuing his own press statement. He argued that there was in fact no
split in the community corresponding to the split in the Executive, and
that support for what he called the 'Memani faction' was 'minimal'.
He also publicly stated that Memani had in fact been expelled from
the Executive. Ngxobongwana's general attitude towards the issue is
captured in his statement:

> He must not cry far from his father and his mother. He should
> come and face his father Ngxobongwana. It is no use to cry on
> the other side of the mountain. I will listen to my son and if I can
> solve his problem I will do so.[32]

From this point onwards a cold war existed between Executive
members loyal to one leader or another. The struggle of each group to
gain political and economic control over both Old and New
Crossroads would continue for some time.

From the beginning of 1982, Ngxobongwana's newly constituted Executive went on the offensive. This was in response to Memani's attempts to develop a support group outside the community. Memani supporters actively campaigned against Ngxobongwana and the Executive, especially amongst organisations such as the Quakers, Women's Movement for Peace, and the Western Province Council of Churches. This had the effect of forcing Ngxobongwana on to the offensive, intensifying already existing divisions.

One of Ngxobongwana's first attempts to discredit Memani and whittle down possible support for his 'Executive' was a lawyer's letter which he sent to Mr Basson, the superintendent at the Nyanga Administration Board offices, and the local official directly responsible for the day to day administration of Crossroads. Richman, well aware of the leadership conflict in Crossroads, no longer acted as their lawyer. The letter is worth quoting:

> We are instructed that the Crossroads [Executive] is an official body, elected by, and representing the people of Crossroads and convened for the purposes of attending to their interests inasfar as they are able. Further we believe that such a Committee has a tacit recognition by your Board and that they have consulted with yourselves for the purpose of discussing various matters relating to the community. We are advised that in recent months a certain amount of friction has developed in the committee. As a result, thereof, a majority of the said committee has seen it fit to expel one, Mr Memani, from the committee in question. We have been instructed by our clients to advise your Board accordingly of such an expulsion . . . .[33]

The next grouping Ngxobongwana and his supporters tried to win over to their side were outside organisations with a long history of involvement in the community. Since the Executive's split in 1981, most organisations had been wary of giving suppport to either Ngxobongwana or Memani. Out of twenty-three welfare and service agencies invited to a meeting in March, only seven attended.[34] After the meeting, at which one committee member after another gave reasons for Memani's expulsion, the Executive issued a press statement. It was intended to explain to a wider audience why the meeting had been called:

> The reason that made us to call this meeting was that we have
> been hearing for some time that many people have questions
> about what is taking place in Crossroads and we wanted to be
> able to explain how things happened and answer the questions
> people have. As residents we are unhappy with people listening
> to rumours and stories from people who do not really know
> what is taking place in our community.[35]

In the light of future developments the most important grouping
that Ngxobongwana and his Executive tried to gain credibility with
were the township-based community organisations. Memani had for
some time been telling them that Ngxobongwana was in fact a community councillor. Although it was true that he was somewhat in-
consistent in his attitude and dealings with local officials, there was no
evidence to substantiate such allegations in 1982.

Ngxobongwana, on hearing about these allegations, which came at
the same time as rumours that the Executive was not sympathetic to
other squatter struggles taking place at the time — for example, the
Nyanga Bush struggle — invited representatives from these organisations to a meeting in Old Crossroads. This took place in March.
Making the best of his oratorical skills, Ngxobongwana had little
trouble in convincing those present that he saw the struggles of Crossroads as part of the broader struggle of black people in the Western
Cape. As a result of this meeting, Ngxobongwana's Executive became
drawn into discussions to consider the formation of a civic organisation in the region. Although the discussions had been going on for
some time, it was only after this meeting that the people of Crossroads
became a part of the process. A month later, Ngxobongwana was
elected the first chairman of this body — the Western Cape Civic
Association (WCCA).

By the middle of 1982 it appeared as though Ngxobongwana and his
new Executive had weathered the storm of internal splits and power
struggles. The cold war with Memani, however, continued. There was
only one known occasion when Ngxobongwana and Memani appeared
to see eye to eye. This occurred in December when vendors' stalls in
the market-place bordering Nyanga East were destroyed by BAAB
officials. The two of them momentarily buried their differences to
issue a joint press statement condemning this action. If they shared
anything, it was a concern for the viability of local business inside the
community. Both blamed local officials for using the leadership split

to destroy the community.

> The so-called split of the Crossroads Committee must no longer be an excuse when it comes to the solution of Crossroads problems by the committees and the local authorities. The members of the committee have come to an agreement to stand up and work together as a united body.[36]

As the events of the next year would show, however, the forces working against this unity were already too great. Before much longer the cold war would break out into the worst violence ever to take place inside Old Crossroads. When this occurred, the struggles of Crossroads were already complicated by other developments taking place in the Cape Peninsula. Before looking at these, it is necessary to see what happened to the women of Crossroads in the years between Koornhof's intervention and the outbreak of conflict.

Notes

1. New Crossroads, Interview No. 2 (1986).
2. Ibid.
3. Although there is little concrete evidence thus far to substantiate it, many residents feel that Ngxobongwana was in some way responsible for Mdayi leaving Crossroads at this time. He was one of a number of people who moved to KTC in the hope of obtaining a house in one of the townships. KTC was seen as a transit camp for legal squatters.
4. Wallace Mgoqi, Joe Ndiki (VERITAS); and Simon Dyakala (Guguletu).
5. New Crossroads, Interview No. 2 (1986).
6. Khayelitsha, Interview (1985).
7. The Sizamile school, for example, fought against Executive control until early 1980. The school consistently remained a rallying point for an anti-Ngxobongwana grouping inside the community until it was burnt down in 1983.
8. New Crossroads, Interview No. 2 (1986).
9. Jane Yanta, Lillian Peter, and Elizabeth Lutango.
10. James Nontulo and Lawrence Kumalo, both Sizamile supporters, died in the November fight.
11. Joint Committee Meeting,'Unofficial Minutes', 7.5.1979.
12. Conflict within state departments was very real. This was especially true at the level of local bureaucracies. Most were under the control of Verwoerdian bureacrats and therefore openly resistant to Koornhof's new 'verligte' initiatives.
13. Johnson Ngxobongwana, Joint Committee Meeting, 'Unofficial Minutes', 7.5.1979.
14. Athlone Advice Office Reports, for the period May — June 1979, show an increased rate of retrenchment of 'illegal' workers during this period. Many Crossroads residents lost their jobs.

15. *Cape Times*, 7.7.1979.
16. Johnson Ngxobongwana, Joint Committee Meeting, 'Unofficial Minutes', 11.7.1979.
17. 'Unofficial Minutes', Noxolo, Crossroads, 14.7.1979.
18. Ibid.
19. *Cape Times*, 24.1.1980.
20. Ibid., 31.1.1980.
21. 'Unofficial Minutes', Noxolo, Crossroads, 14.2.1980.
22. *Cape Times*, 20.10.1979.
23. Ibid., 20.11.1979.
24. This letter, dated 12.12.1979, was personally signed by Timo Bezuidenhoud.
25. Letter from the Crossroads Executive to the Department of Community Development, dated 13.12.1979.
26. New Crossroads, Interview No. 2 (1986).
27. *Cape Times*, 19.2.1981.
28. Ibid., 28.2.1981.
29. 'Memorandum on Crossroads', September 1981.
30. *Cape Times*, 22.9.1981.
31. Old Crossroads, Interview (1981).
32. *Argus*, 29.9.1981.
33. Letter, I.M. Russell, Movsowitz and Kahn, to Mr Basson, dated 27.1.1982.
34. New Crossroads, Interview (1985).
35. 'Unofficial Minutes', Noxolo, 23.3.1982.
36. *Cape Times*, 18.12.1982.

Chapter 4

The Defeat of the Women

A significant feature of Crossroads early history is the central role women played in both its formation and defence. This was directly related to specific social and political pressures which impinged upon the lives of African women in the Western Cape — especially during the late 1960s and early 1970s. To understand the history, which at its most fundamental level is one of ongoing resistance to the migrant labour system and influx control, and therefore a working class struggle, one needs to incorporate women's struggles. Crossroads women's experiences were different to the men's. In addition to struggles against the state and capital, these women often found themselves battling against patriarchal attitudes inside their own community. In the months and years immediately following Koornhof's intervention and the rise of a male-dominated bureaucratic elite in Crossroads, the women would find themselves removed from positions of organised power in the community. Their defeat was as significant as their entry into the politics of the community.

Imfuduso — 'The Exodus'

When Koornhof first visited Crossroads in November 1978, the Women's Committee was busy rehearsing a play which had developed in the aftermath of the September raids. While most of the community, as well as the Noxolo and Sizamile Committees, were physically and emotionally overwhelmed by the strain of the year's events, the women responded creatively to the crisis. This was something they were used to doing.

Imfuduso arose out of discussions among members of the Women's Committee following the raids. The play they created was a sustained reflection on how women experienced life before, and while, living at

Crossroads. This is how one of the women described why they had
decided to create the play:

> We the women of Crossroads have a little sketch. The way we
> are looking at Crossroads we started thinking deep that people
> must see how we are living . . . . We started thinking where we
> came from . . . the bushes we came from before we came to
> Crossroads. We've always been thinking what we could do
> about this . . . because we are not happy all the time . . . .
> That's why we thought of this sketch . . . to teach us and show
> what we are . . . . Whether things can happen to us we've still
> got hope. That's why we called it *Imfuduso* — the Exodus . . . .
> This little sketch is going to be a remembrance of how we are
> thinking in Crossroads.[1]

In many ways *Imfuduso* symbolised a growing proto-feminist consciousness on the part of some of these women. The fact that it was
women who created and acted both the male and female roles in the
play was indicative of perceptions many Crossroads women had then,
and continue to have up to this day, that the struggle to remain in the
Western Cape was, essentially, a women's struggle. One of the women
who took part in the play expressed this in the following way:

> We had no men in the play because we felt it was really us — the
> women — who were really feeling the pain. We were the ones
> who did fight for Crossroads. If the government [state officials]
> came the men would run away. But a woman, she won't give in
> so easily . . . . What made us to be strong was that we really
> suffered . . . .[2]

It was in the midst of rehearsals for the opening performance of the
play at The Space theatre in Cape Town that Koornhof announced his
'reprieve' for Crossroads. The women had no idea that his politics of
reform would help pave the way for intensified struggles with the men
of Crossroads.

Gender Politics

Although women took part in the Koornhof negotiations, they by no
means played a leading role. Richman and Wilson, for example, often

met with Waka and Ngxobongwana without representatives of the Women's Committee being present. The final weeks of the negotiations were also complicated by the fact that a large number of members from the Women's Committee were on tour in Johannesburg with *Imfuduso*.[3] Members of the committee unsuccessfully tried to persuade Richman and Wilson to postpone any final decisions until they returned to Crossroads. Jane Yanta and Regina Ntongana, the two women representatives on the negotiating team, were eventually forced to fly back to Cape Town so as not to miss 'crucial' meetings on 1 April with the UF and Koornhof.

Members of the Women's Committee were as confused about whether or not to trust Koornhof as were the men. They were also equally divided. Women who expressed reservations found themselves as marginalised as outsiders who did. As a result the Women's Committee representatives 'acquiesced' along with the men of Noxolo and Sizamile. Like them, they saw no other way of staying in Crossroads.

> We did negotiate with [Koornhof] simply because we were desperate. We didn't have a chance to think. I, myself, I really did think he was going to help us. But there were many things that made me doubt . . . . We were really confused. We did trust what he said but we did know that his officials were not satisfied with what was taking place. We did know then that it wouldn't be easy to succeed in what Dr Koornhof promised us . . . .[4]

In the months immediately following the Koornhof settlement, women continued to take part in community discussions — for example, about the survey. They were particularly suspicious about some of the questions being asked, and participated fully in the decision not to accept the proposed questionnaire. When the survey eventually took place (July — August), women were part of the twenty Joint Committee members who accompanied BAAB officials in the field. They were also implicated in the fraud and corruption which accompanied the selling of temporary permits. A woman who now lives in New Crossroads remembers this period with some bitterness:

> The officials did bribe at this time, simply because they were used to that. They always did this at the Nyanga and Langa offices. It wasn't something new to us . . . . They even came at

night to people's houses . . . . Having meetings and selling permits while we were sleeping. In the daytime they were making
braais with the people and I don't know what else. Crossroads
was just like a farm to them . . . .[5]

Co-operation with local officials came with its own price. In the
long term, it was no less important in undermining the strength of the
Women's Committee than the political manoeuvres of some of the
men in the Noxolo and Sizamile committees. For a long time women
had known that some men were unhappy with their political role in the
community. They had learned to live with this in the course of earlier
struggles (1975-1978) when women had constantly to battle against
traditional views which saw politics as the realm of men. Women had
taken the lead despite this criticism because, as they so often stated, it
was they who really 'felt the pain'. Their entry into politics was directly
related to their experiences of life and struggle. As squatters *and*
women, politics underscored every aspect of their lives. Challenging
the men was not easy.

The men were feeling that the women were so strong [and] that
they were made to feel helpless. They were unhappy because
according to custom a woman doesn't have the right to do
something in public without consulting a man. We didn't care
what the men said . . . . And they said a lot. But we wanted to
help our people . . . . And this custom thing, it is a terrible
thing. Sometimes there is a big problem in the house. [You] as a
woman you try to give advice. But for the sake that he is a black
man he won't accept what you have to say. Except if you force
things, then he has to listen. It isn't that you don't respect him.
It is just that you are trying to show that what you think or feel
about something is as good as a man, sometimes better. But it
isn't an easy thing.[6]

Before 1979, this ongoing struggle between men and women had to
a large degree been hidden by broader issues affecting Crossroads. At
the same moment that the state began its more sophisticated strategies
of divide and rule, men in Crossroads went on the offensive. When
Waka and Ngxobongwana mobilised for one chairman and one central committee, they purposefully excluded the women. The women
were completely taken by surprise.

4 *Members of the Crossroads Women's Committee (left to right): Mrs Maphisa, Mrs Nkondweni, Mrs Ntongana, Mrs Luke, Mrs Tom, Mrs Mewe; Mrs Peter (front).*

5 *Crossroads women protest against frequent 'crime prevention' raids in front of the Administration Board offices in Goodwood (June 1978).*

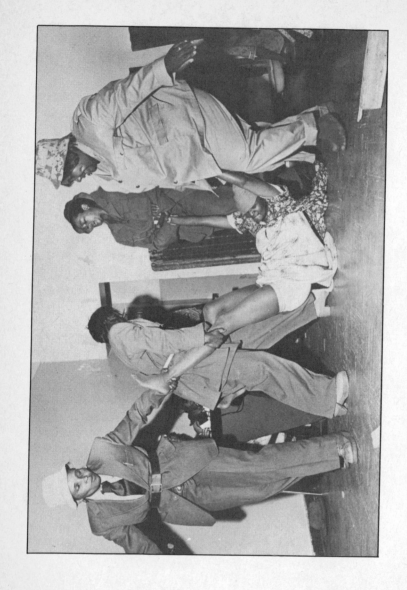

6 A scene from the women's play, Imfuduso, during a performance in Soweto (March 1979).

We don't know how it did happen, but the men decided to have one committee and kick the women away. They did know that the women were brighter and stronger and they didn't want it to be like this. They wanted to just grab everything. Now all of a sudden they were the people who went to Koornhof and all over the place. They put us behind and we did sit down. And we were fed up, because really nothing was happening. Everything the officials told them they just agreed. When the officials put them in a tight corner, they just agreed. It would never have been like that if the women was involved. No easy agreements if women was there. Things must be laid on the table. The men didn't want us at meetings simply because they knew they did make mistakes. And they knew we wouldn't just accept it easy . . . . They wanted everything. All of a sudden they were the Executive, the Working Committee, the Appeal Committee, the School Committee, [and] the Crèche Committee. And things can't be like that. You must have other committees to do all these things. They [also] didn't explain things to the people like before. And the people were getting lost . . . . When I look deep into things it was this thing that brought all the corruption to Crossroads . . . .[7]

The elections of 1979 removed decision-making from women leaders in the community. The Women's Committee, effectively 'banned' from having meetings at the Noxolo community hall where it had met every Wednesday afternoon, was forced to revert to earlier patterns of mobilisation and organisation — open air gatherings. Criticism of the Executive was forced underground. Regina Ntongana, whose husband was secretary of the Executive, remembers these as being difficult times.

It was a difficult time in my house in those days. There were days [when my husband and I] weren't speaking. And the women were also looking at me to see which way I would blow . . . . I can say it was almost divorce.[8]

The undermining of the women's power was reinforced by the actions of local state officials. Timo Bezuidenhoud, for example, never missed an opportunity to drive a wedge between the men and women of Crossroads. On one occasion when members of the

Women's Committee visited him at his office in town, desperate to find out what was being decided about the new township, he lost no time in telling the Executive that they had come to see him. His actions helped to fuel already existing tensions between the two groups.[9]

The women were acutely aware that Executive members were being co-opted by local officials and that, in the process, community cohesion was being slowly weakened.

> They [the officials] tried to make us weak . . . . One of the first things they did was to give jobs to some Executive members in the Administration Board. And the men couldn't see what was taking place. Although they did know they were from Crossroads, it made it difficult for them to know where they really were . . . .[10]

Bezuidenhoud and his officials, confident that they were working with a leadership in Crossroads which could easily be co-opted, continued unchallenged with divisive strategies. These objectives coincided with those of a willing sector of men only too eager to keep women in their 'place'. Between them, they were able to defuse the most militant and politically astute social grouping in Crossroads at the time — the women. They did not realise that, in doing so, they were weakening their struggle as a whole. Crossroads women did not, however, capitulate without a bitter struggle.

Attempts To Re-organise

In the last few months of 1980, the women began to go on the offensive. They mobilised general community support around the issue of the proposed move to New Crossroads. They successfully pressurised the Executive into calling a mass meeting to discuss a number of issues around the move. At the meeting leaders of the Women's Committee spoke from the floor as part of the general community. Women were strategically placed in the community hall as part of the overall plan to gain control of the meeting. The issues under discussion were the kinds of housing being offered at the new township, and who would teach in the schools. The women were not satisfied with the way in which local officials were making decisions — largely without consulting the community — nor were they impressed with the role of the

Executive. This meeting was intended to provide them with an opportunity to voice their opinions and influence the direction of the
Executive Committee. After eighteen months of relative quiescence,
the women were once again on the offensive.

> We decided as women to stand up, never mind what, simply
> because we could see that things were never going to come right.
> Everything was just left. Even the houses in New Crossroads
> that was built. The men agreed to houses with no chimneys in
> the kitchen and doors that opened the wrong way. Even our
> teachers didn't get jobs in the new schools like Dr Koornhof
> promised . . . . We went to the new schools and we closed them.
> Never mind it was a legal government school, we just locked it
> up. We forced the authorities to put things right and really in the
> end we did get our teachers into the schools like we wanted.[11]

After it became clear to the Executive that they needed the support
of the women they allowed the Women's Committee to operate openly,
but things were never again the same. The women of Crossroads were
not able to regain the political position they had once held. In addition
to obstacles put in their way by the Executive, there were visible divisions amongst the women themselves. The fact that a number of key
leaders moved from Old to New Crossroads in the course of 1980-1981
put added burdens on maintaining solidarity. Although, in the early
days of resettlement, Regina Ntongana tried on numerous occasions
to hold meetings with Women's Committee members in New and Old
Crossroads, women did not see this as a priority. A number of them
also began to express the same petit-bourgeois aspirations as the
Executive. As a result, the solidarity of the women began to crumble
from within.

> When people moved [1980-1981] we lost more spirit — even the
> women — because some of the leaders moved to that side. We
> used to run from one side to the other trying to get [the women]
> together but all of a sudden they became like the men. Some
> became 'Mrs My-house'. They were also losing power, fighting
> amongst themselves and forgetting about the real struggle in
> front of us. I think the women were also a little bit tired after
> what happened when the men took over. The women lost power,
> so it was easy for them to fight amongst themselves.[12]

Nomzamo — She Who Struggles

During the emergence of township-based community organisations in
the early 1980s, various attempts were made to bring the women of
Old Crossroads — still under the leadership of Regina Ntongana —
closer to newly developing women's organisations. This did not prove
to be an easy task. When a number of former members of the
Women's Federation were trying to mobilise support for a political
women's organisation in the Western Cape they asked to address a
Women's Committee general meeting. The women were from nearby
Nyanga and Guguletu. At the meeting they were confronted by considerable resistance. Although some of the leaders were keen to make
direct links with more overtly political organisations, rank and file
members were on the whole reluctant to do so. Many women in
Crossroads felt that the township women were not able to offer them
anything.

> When they came to Crossroads that year [1981] some of the
> women were against this. They said that the township women
> weren't strong and also they were never with us in our struggle.
> They said now they want to come and lead us, for us to be
> behind them. We wanted to show them that we were also strong.
> Some of us we did understand. We did feel, alright, they weren't
> strong when we were in a corner, but it is time for us to stand up
> in the Western Cape as women. The township women were there
> in the sixties but they had it so hard. They just couldn't stand
> any more. It's not to say they didn't care, but a lot of people
> were scared. As I see it people also didn't know then what the
> struggle is all about. They weren't really clear. People didn't
> have a strong platform and that's why they sat down. I did try to
> show the women that we must stay close to the township women
> and then fight together for one thing. But I had it hard from the
> Crossroads women . . . .[13]

This ambivalence towards women's political organisations would
remain for a long time. It was to some extent based on the sense that
their struggle was qualitatively different from that of the women of
Guguletu and Nyanga. They felt that many of them had not
undergone the same kinds of struggles as the Crossroads women.

It would remain an ongoing struggle for women's political organisations to gain the confidence of Crossroads women. When the women of Old Crossroads attempted once again to reorganise (1980), they chose to do so not as part of, or with the assistance of, other women's organisations. Instead they established their own organisation — *Nomzamo*.

This was the first, and last, attempt by the Crossroads women to establish an organisation, as opposed to a committee, inside the community. It was established for a number of reasons. Firstly, many of the women were critical of the leadership struggles taking place between Memani and Ngxobongwana. The ongoing political power struggles meant that many community issues — for example, people who still had not obtained residence permits — were not being attended to. The Executive's main concern appeared to be the accumulation of capital. This they did through a variety of community 'taxes', administered and collected by headmen in the area. The formation of *Nomzamo* was an attempt to intervene in this process. It was also seen as a way to re-establish links with women who had moved to New Crossroads. One of the aims was to establish a branch there and have women from both Old and New Crossroads represented on a central committee structure. In essence the launching of a new women's organisation, as opposed to a committee, was an attempt to re-involve women in community issues and, in the process, democratise the politics of Crossroads.

The women's organisation was not, however, able to overcome the deep divisions already firmly entrenched in the community. Within six months of its formation, *Nomzamo* had disintegrated. It became impossible to hold out a vision of democracy within a commmunity that was essentially already being run like a mini-bantustan. Women found themselves caught up in the power struggles of Memani and Ngxobongwana, as well as struggles over economic resources within their own organisation. When violent conflicts took place between Memani and Ngxobongwana supporters in 1983, Crossroads women were as active in the conflict as the men. This proved to be the end of their active participation, *as leaders*, in determining Crossroads' history. Although the women of Crossroads would re-emerge in the future, their role would be qualitatively different from what it had been in the past.

Notes

1. Old Crossroads, Interview (1978).
2. Old Crossroads, Interview No. 3 (1984).
3. *Imfuduso* played at the Market Theatre for a week at the end of March 1979.
4. Old Crossroads, Interview No. 3 (1984).
5. Ibid.
6. Ibid.
7. Ibid.
8. Regina Ntongana, Interview (Old Crossroads, 1983).
9. Ibid. When the women were excluded from attending meetings in late 1979 and 1980, especially concerning the rentals and housing development proposed for New Crossroads, they initially accepted that decision-making was, in effect, out of their hands. When they felt that it was necessary to intervene — at the time that there was general confusion in the minds of the residents as to whether or not they should move into the new houses — the Women's Committee decided to go and see Bezuidenhoud to find out exactly what the position was. Within hours of the women's visit to his office in town, Bezuidenhoud phoned the Executive to inform them of their visit. He was well aware at the time that this would create problems between the Executive and the Women's Committee.
10. Ibid.
11. Old Crossroads, Interview No. 2 (1984).
12. Regina Ntongana, Interview (Old Crossroads 1983).
13. Old Crossroads, Interview No. 5 (1984).

Chapter 5

A Squatter 'Problem' Becomes a Squatter 'Crisis'

The policy of influx control is being scientifically applied, with the chief vision of placing blacks in service, organising the provision of labour, and consolidating it with supply and demand.[1]

During the early 1980s when, as we have seen, the leaders and residents of Old and New Crossroads concerned themselves with particularist community issues and internal power struggles, events were taking place in the Cape Peninsula which eventually forced them to relate to the broader struggles. This began in early 1981, as one group of squatters after another began to occupy land adjacent to New and Old Crossroads. Faced with these new developments, Koornhof responded with a combination of reform and repression. When arrests and deportations proved ineffective in dealing with a growing squatter crisis in the Cape, he eventually came up with what he considered to be an overall solution to the crisis — a new township for all 'legal' residents in the Cape Peninsula (Khayelitsha). This announcement in March 1983 signalled the suspension of his original promises to the residents of Old and New Crossroads. It also precipitated a crisis for the thousands of 'illegal' squatters in the area. The state's strategy would force the Ngxobongwana leadership to seek a tactical alliance with the surrounding squatter communities *and* a growing progressive movement in their struggle to resist removal. With the formation of the United Democratic Front (UDF) in 1983, the objective conditions were present for squatter resistance to become highly politicised. Old Crossroads, led by Ngxobongwana, once again found itself at the forefront of resistance.

The Crisis Begins — Nyanga Extension (Emavundleni)

The growth of the new squatter settlements had its roots in a clearance programme begun by Bezuidenhoud's department as early as October 1979. This was part of a generalised attempt by the state to tighten up influx control. Koornhof had made it exceedingly clear with his April settlement that allowing certain Crossroads residents to stay did not mean that squatter control was over. The squatter clearance which began in 1979 was not unlike the one that had taken place in 1974. The immediate effect of the 1974 clearance was, as we have seen, the formation of Crossroads and other settlements — Unibel, Werkgenot and Modderdam. This pattern of relocating, rather than solving the problem, was repeated in the course of the 1980s when hundreds of 'illegal' African squatters were forcibly removed from areas such as Hout Bay, Killarney and Tableview.[2] 'Legal' squatters from these areas were temporarily housed in single-sex hostels in Langa (barracks) and told that they could remain there while their cases were being 'investigated'. Before long others, considered 'illegal', joined the Langa squatters. There they remained until threatened with removal in early 1981. The project of a reform-minded employer to renovate and turn the barracks into family housing units precipitated a crisis for the inhabitants. In late March BAAB officials and police raided the barracks, arresting hundreds of squatters. To make sure that none would return, they sealed the barracks off.[3] As a result many became refugees. They were given a place to stay at a nearby church in Langa.[4]

After a week there, the squatters, assisted by church and community workers from the Quakers and Women's Movement for Peace, adopted a different strategy. They moved onto unoccupied land along Lansdowne Road, next to the Old Crossroads squatter camp. With the memory of the Crossroads 'reprieve' still fresh in their minds, they settled there hoping eventually to receive permission to stay. They were determined to struggle for the right to live and work in the Western Cape. Some claimed that local officials had encouraged them to move to 'the bush'.

I came here in 1981 because they demolished Zone 24 in Langa. We went to the Langa offices to ask for a place to stay. Mr Lawrence [a BAAB official] told us to go and stay in the bush. We stayed here until they arrested . . . and deported us to Umtata . . . .[5]

After a two-month struggle which included arrests and unsuccessful

deportations of squatters to the Transkei, the state was forced to con-
cede defeat.[6] The authorities agreed to negotiate. After a meeting in
June with a number of representatives of the squatters,[7] Koornhof
offered the group (approximately 200 people) Section 10 1 (d) permits
and the right to erect 83 shacks on the Mahobe Drive side of Old
Crossroads, next to the WCDB offices. This squatter settlement, first
called Emavundleni, then Bez's Valley, eventually became known as
Nyanga Extension. The leader of this settlement was Issac Gwiliza.
What Koornhof did not realise, however, was that this group of squatters merely represented the tip of a much larger iceberg. Within less
than two weeks he was faced with a new and much greater crisis — the
Nyanga Bush struggle.

Esgangeni — Nyanga Bush

In mid-July between 1000 and 2000 squatters moved onto land a few
hundred yards from the newly established Nyanga Extension camp.
The majority came from Langa where renovations to the 'zones' were
still taking place. Koornhof's initial response, carried out by his local
officials, was one of total repression. Within a matter of hours after
their arrival on 13 July, police raided the settlement. They arrested
over a thousand people.[8]

An important feature of this particular struggle was the support it
received from individuals and organisations based in the African
townships. Prior to this, the only groups involved in squatter 'issues'
had been the churches and liberal organisations. By 1981, with the
growth of new organisations and the trade union movement in the
Cape Peninsula, the situation was no longer the same. When the
squatters appeared at the Langa Commissioner's court the following
day, they were given support by over 1000 squatters who had escaped
arrest, as well as hundreds of residents from the surrounding
townships. This support was not readily accepted by the squatters'
leaders, known as the Bush Committee.

These leaders had built up strong relationships with community and
church workers from the WPCC and the Quakers prior to moving onto the site. For reasons not clearly known, some of the community
workers were critical of the township-based activists and community
organisations.[9] Two mass meetings were held in the townships at
which 43 community organisations and trade unions pledged and

offered support to the Nyanga Bush squatters. The Bush Committee, however, categorically rejected the support offered to them by what they considered to be 'political' organisations. With little experience in the realm of squatter struggles and no material resources to offer the people, activists found themselves marginalised and, as a result, unable to sustain any meaningful intervention during this period.[10] It would take a few more years before community organisations could actively intervene and influence squatter struggles in the Cape Peninsula. When they did so, this support was not without its own contradictions.

After weeks of continuous raids, resistance, and adverse local and international publicity, Koornhof tried a different strategy. On 14 August, he announced that some of the squatters were to have their presence legalised. Others were offered jobs in the Orange Free State and Transvaal. No new jobs were to be created in the Western Cape and no squatting was to be allowed, even on a temporary basis, at Nyanga Bush. Workers who accepted the offer would not be allowed to take their families with them. The women and children of Nyanga Bush were expected to return to the homelands.[11] This offer was rejected outright by the Bush Committee who refused to be divided. They demanded 'passes and places to stay' — in the Western Cape.

Koornhof's offer was publicised far and wide through the press and radio. The SABC, for example, announced that 500 of the jobs were in agriculture and 600 in mining. Even though these were traditionally the worst jobs, the size of Nyanga Bush's population tripled within the space of a few days[12] as thousands of homeless people joined the camp in the hope of finding both jobs and accommodation. Some people alleged that the 'wireless' and local officials had encouraged them to do so. The state responded with a major raid on the settlement in the early hours of 19 August, in which an estimated 2000 squatters were arrested and taken to Pollsmoor Prison. There they were separated into 'Transkei' and 'Ciskei' citizens. Squatters classified as 'Transkeians' were immediately put on railway buses and deported to the capital of 'independent' Transkei — Umtata — in terms of the Aliens Act. This was the first instance when this Act was used to remove 'illegal' squatters from South Africa.[13]

Koornhof made clear his position on the Nyanga Bush squatters when he announced in the press that as far as his department was concerned, the only way to deal with squatting was to 'nip it in the bud as soon as it [reared] its ugly head'.[14] His threat was given substance when roadblocks were set up throughout the Western Cape in an attempt to stop the deported squatters from returning. This proved ineffective. Within a few days of the arrests and deportations, the press reported that there were over 900 squatters on their way back to the Western Cape.[15] Getting rid of the Nyanga Bush squatters was not going to be an easy task.

The fact that the state used Transkei's 'independence' to divide the arrested squatters into Ciskei and Transkei 'citizens', and deport the latter as 'aliens', had the effect of creating two distinct groups. One, led by Mali Hoza, the leader of the Bush Committee, consisted of those left behind in Cape Town. Their rural linkages were not necessarily 'Ciskeian'. The other group, led by Melford Yamile, consisted of those classified 'Transkeian' by the South African state. During their two-month stay in church halls in Umtata, Yamile's group developed into a relatively cohesive squatter community.[16] Their common experiences in Umtata gave them a sense of being a group separate from those who remained behind in Cape Town under the leadership of the Bush Committee. In late October, when the Yamile group returned to Cape Town with the assistance of the Transkei government, they chose to return to the bush rather than the townships like the other squatters. They did this against the wishes of the Bush Committee. From this time onwards Yamile's group, now called the Sand Dune squatters, were treated as 'dissidents' by the Bush Committee and their supporters. As soon as the squatters returned to the bush they were subjected to intensive raids and arrests.

In Umtata Matanzima said we [couldn't] stay there because we belonged to the government of the Cape . . . . He said we couldn't stay there, people with lice and people who are ragged. He asked the Cape government to send money and when [they] sent the money we came back to the Cape . . . we started again to go back to Mr Lawrence. Before we went there we went to the church of Fr. Curran but he chased us away. He said he didn't care for people who came from the Transkei. We thought what to do and went to Langa again to ask for passes and places to stay. Mr Lawrence chased us away. He said that if we weren't gone within 5 minutes he would have us taken away. We went away and started this new bush. That was the 10th of November . . . . We stay here very hard. There were about 500 of us but the police chased us away . . . . Now we are only left with about 300.[17]

7   *An evening prayer service at Esgangeni (Nyanga Bush) (July 1981).*

8   *One of many police raids — Esgangeni (August 1981).*

9   *54 families fast at St George's Cathedral, Cape Town (March 1982).*

From November 1981, the Sand Dune squatters, described by Bezuidenhoud as 'a hard core of about 300 people who ignore everything we say and keep coming back',[18] fought a protracted and largely hidden battle against local police and WCAB officials to remain on the land. The camp was raided constantly in the first half of 1982. The Sand Dune squatters refused to leave the area and actively sought the help of progressive church and community organisations. In March, following a solidarity meeting for the Nyanga Bush squatters in Old Crossroads, a support committee was elected. The Nyanga Bush Action Committee, as this group was called, tried to gain the support of the Bush Committee but with no success.[19] With the two groups so divided, the Action Committee found itself unable to offer any meaningful support. Any hopes of re-uniting the two groups were dashed when the Hoza group, without letting anyone other than a select few know, moved into St.George's Cathedral to begin a fast. This action on the part of the Bush Committee and their supporters signalled the official split amongst the Nyanga Bush squatters. From March 1982 onwards, Hoza's group were known as the Cathedral Group squatters. Their strategies of resistance were qualitatively different from those of the Sand Dune squatters. Unlike this group, they never chose to align themselves with the embryonic progressive movement in the Cape Peninsula.

Hoza's group, with the support of church and community workers, and without seeking the support of community-based organisations or residents from the surrounding black townships, many of whom were keen to show solidarity with the Nyanga Bush struggle, started their fast in early March. The event received a vast amount of local and international publicity and support. Koornhof was forced to respond.

In early April he entered into negotiations with the squatters, promising to investigate their situation *provided* they called off their fast and moved out of the Cathedral. This they agreed to do, after Koornhof gave them permission to stay temporarily at Holy Cross church, Nyanga. The squatters stayed there until the middle of June when Koornhof gave them permission to move onto land between the Sand Dune squatters and the Nyanga Extension camp. There the WCAB provided them with tents and temporary toilets. By the middle of 1982 there were three squatter communities living on land adjacent to the Old Crossroads camp — the Sand Dune squatters, the Cathedral Group, and Nyanga Extension.

Within days of the Cathedral Group moving to their new site, local

officials carried out a survey to ascertain the number of people living
in both Hoza's and Yamile's groups. After this, 3-month permits were
issued to all the adults living in the camps. Although there were an
estimated 3000 squatters living in both camps, only 737 received the
temporary permits. These were valid until 20 September 1982.
Bezuidenhoud promised the squatters that by the time the permits
expired in September, he would tell the squatters what decision his
department had decided upon. On 20 September, he issued a press
statement spelling out the government's position on the fate of the
'illegal' squatters:

> Earlier this year the government informed you that your
> position would be thoroughly examined and that you would be
> informed on [today] as to what could be done regarding your
> position. It is a fact that in terms of relevant laws of the country,
> many of you are here illegally. Furthermore it is a fact that many
> of you are in the Peninsula due to circumstances beyond your
> control. It is also a fact that as squatters you are living under
> deplorable conditions. The government fully appreciates these
> facts and is therefore consulting with all parties concerned to
> arrive at a better dispensation for the Nyanga squatters . . . . It
> must be clearly understood that in the meantime the government
> will not allow your ranks to be strengthened from outside.
> Sterner measures will therefore be taken against those people
> who come to the Peninsula without the necessary authority. By
> the same token firm action will be taken against those employers
> who engage or retain the services of people in contravention of
> legal requirements. As far as possible cases of merit will be
> accommodated. For those who cannot be accommodated, the
> government is actively engaged to bring about a dispensation
> whereby they will be accommodated elsewhere on a family basis
> and provided with work. This is the only way in which the
> squatter problem can be dealt with and a better dispensation be
> provided for the squatters of Nyanga.[20]

On the same day the state announced that 4000 squatters awaiting
twelve-month permits in Old Crossroads did not qualify in terms of
the Koornhof settlement of 1979. The fate of all 'illegal' squatters in
the Cape Peninsula still hung in the balance. There were no real solutions offered by the state despite the fact that as early as 1981 local

WCAB officials were acknowledging that the housing backlog in the Cape had reached critical proportions. There was little likelihood that any of the squatters would return to the homelands. In 1982, the percentage of the population 'illegally' resident in the Western Cape was being conservatively estimated at well over 40%.[21] The only solution the state could offer was the Orderly Movement and Settlement of Black Person's Bill. It was introduced by Koornhof in late 1982.

The Bill, an extension of the Riekert Proposals of 1979, attempted to decrease the mobility and access of Africans to the urban areas and restrict permanent residence to a small elite. It also introduced tighter controls over squatting in both the urban areas and on white farms. Section 31 of the Bill dealt specifically with squatters:

> If any Black persons settle in such numbers on a piece of land to which they have no right and reside on that land in such conditions from which it appears in the opinion of the minister that their conduct is:
>
> a) calculated to canvass support for a campaign for the repeal, or amendment, of any law, or for the variation of the limitation of the application of the law;
>
> b) is calculated to endanger the maintenance of law and order;
>
> c) threatens their own health, the social welfare, or the health of the public in general:
>
> The minister may by notice in the gazette order that any Black person who on, or after, a date stated in the notice, is unlawfully resident on that land . . . may be summarily removed with his dependents (if any) to the area from which he comes in the opinion of the director general or to any other place or area indicated by the latter . . . .[22]

The Bill was condemned by organised business, commerce, churches, community and international bodies. As a result of this outcry, Koornhof was forced to withdraw it during the 1982 parliamentary session. Faced with no legislative arsenal, a growing economic crisis, growing political mobilisation in the urban areas, and defiant squatter communities in the Cape Peninsula, the state was forced to return to strategies of overt repression. In the latter half of 1982, pass raids were intensified throughout the country, with an emphasis on the Cape. This did not prove a deterrent to squatting in the Cape

Peninsula. In early 1983, another group of squatters 'illegally' occupied land — the KTC squatters. Their struggle would force Koornhof to reformulate solutions in another desperate attempt to eradicate 'illegal' squatting in the Cape Peninsula. Koornhof publicly vowed that 'neither I, nor this government will allow another un-controlled squatter camp like Crossroads to develop'.[23] With time he would learn, along with other members of his party, that squatting was a phenomenon in the Western Cape that could not be so easily wished away.

KTC

During the first few weeks of February, in the midst of intensive raids and harassment, hundreds of plastic shelters were set up on land adjacent to what was known as the KTC squatter camp. The camp had been in existence for years, and consisted of a few thousand legal squatters, all of whom were on the waiting list for housing. KTC was directly opposite the first phase of New Crossroads houses, on land earmarked for Phase 2 of the housing development. A significant feature of the KTC struggle was that a large percentage of those who moved onto the land were township residents who for many years had been waiting for houses. Some had been lodgers and backyard tenants in the surrounding townships. The official housing backlog at the time was estimated at 6000.[24] Hundreds of homeless families began to stream into the area. By the middle of February there were an estimated 400 plastic shelters on the site. The state responded with a series of raids which failed to remove the squatters. Mounting public pressure, together with the tenacious resistance of the squatters, forced Koornhof to step in with one of his by now famous 'deals'. He offered 200 homes to be built on the site for what he called 'the most deserving cases'. A day later, when this was rejected, he offered 2500 sites for the 'legal' lodgers. This offer was followed by intensive raids on the camp. In one such raid, 289 squatters were arrested.[25] Koornhof's divide and rule tactics were not without effect. By March the KTC camp was effectively split into three distinct groups — 'legals', 'illegals', and a mixed group of 'legals and illegals'.

Clearly alarmed by what was becoming a crisis situation, Koornhof and P.W. Botha flew over the black townships and squatter areas in a helicopter to review the situation.[26] Three weeks later Bezuidenhoud

announced that the proposed self-build scheme first offered by
Koornhof had been shelved 'pending the outcome of cabinet-level discussions'.[27] At the end of March, Koornhof announced the state's
latest solution — a 'high density' black township at Swartklip, east of
the 'coloured' township Mitchells Plain. This marked the beginning of
the new housing development, Khayelitsha. It was presented to the
public as a major shift in government policy.[28]

The Khayelitsha proposal was seen by local black residents and outside groups as yet a new form of social control over the black urban
population. It offered no meaningful solution to any residents — legal
or illegal. As a result it was rejected outright by a broad range of community, church and business organisations — including Old
Crossroads which, for the first time since 1978, found itself threatened
with possible resettlement. Of even greater importance, this latest
government strategy came at a time when broad-based extra
parliamentary opposition, on the upswing in South Africa and the
Western Cape, had created the potential for politicising local struggles.
From 1983 onwards, squatter struggles in the Cape Peninsula entered
a qualitatively new historical phase.

For the squatters of KTC, life remained bitter. In May, local
WCAB officials, backed by the South African Police (SAP), dogs,
teargas, and sneeze machines, raided the camp. The raid was met by
youths throwing stones and wielding sticks. Women from the area
marched on the WCAB offices at Goodwood to protest about the
consistent raids. In the middle of May the state made its position un-
equivocally clear as regards the KTC squatters. Spotlights were trained
on the people, making it impossible for them to re-erect their shelters.
Barbed wire was erected around the camp and teargas thrown at
crowds of people who went to the area to show their solidarity with
the squatters.[29] By June all the 'illegal' squatters had been moved from
the area. Many of them sought refuge amongst the Sand Dune squatters. Although it seemed as though the state had successfully removed
the problem of KTC, the squatter crisis in the Cape Peninsula was far
from over. It had merely been relocated.

Notes

1. Piet Koornhof, quoted in *Die Burger*, 23.3.1980.
2. *Cape Times*, 23.2.1980.
3. Ibid. 25.3.1981.

4. St.Cyprian's Anglican Church, Langa.
5. Nyanga Bush, Interview (1984).
6. On 22 May, 55 women and children were deported to the Transkei. They hired a bus and were back on the site within less than a week. See *Cape Times* 22.5.1981.
7. The Western Province Council of Churches, Quakers and Women's Movement for Peace.
8. *Cape Times*, 16.7.1981.
9. One of the community workers, Rommel Roberts, was particularly vociferous on this issue.
10. See NUSAS, *The Nyanga Bush Struggle* (Cape Town, 1981) for more details on why progressive organisations failed in their attempts to intervene in this particular struggle.
11. *Argus*, 14.8.1981.
12. *Cape Times*, 16.8.1981.
13. Aliens Act No. 1 of 1937.
14. *Argus*, 26.8.1981.
15. *Cape Times*, 28.8.1981.
16. A large number stayed at the Catholic Church in Umtata, assisted by the priest, Fr. Dick O' Rioden.
17. Nyanga Bush, Interview (1984).
18. *Cape Times*, 31.1.1982.
19. The Nyanga Bush Action Committee consisted of five people — three township residents, Rev. Sidney Luckett and myself.
20. *Cape Times*, 20.9.1982.
21. See Black Sash Advice Office Report (March, 1982).
22. Quoted from Section 31 of the Orderly Movement and Settlement of Black Persons Bill (1982).
23. *Cape Times*, 19.2.1983.
24. Gert du Preez, WCAB official, quoted in the *Cape Times*, 13.2.1983.
25. *Cape Times*, 25.2.1983.
26. *Hansard*, Col. 61, 25.3.1983.
27. *Cape Times*, 9.3.1983.
28. With the exception of New Crossroads (1980) no family housing units had been built in the Cape Peninsula since 1972.
29. *Cape Times*, 17.5.1983.

Chapter 6

Khayelitsha 'Over our Dead Bodies'

In the course of 1983, following the announcement of Khayelitsha in March, the state pushed forward with a two-pronged strategy to deal with the growing crisis in the Cape Peninsula. Firstly, it began building the first phase of the new township; and secondly, it put pressure on squatters living 'illegally' in the area. Old Crossroads found itself under the same pressure as the surrounding squatter settlements of Nyanga Bush and KTC. As a result of this ongoing and increasing threat of removal, the leadership of Crossroads joined forces with the surrounding camps. Before long they found themselves part of the progressive movement in the Western Cape. The launching of the United Democratic Front (UDF) in August breathed new life into localised struggles. In the Cape Peninsula, the UDF was forced by objective conditions to take up the squatter issue and support their resistance. Ngxobongwana, as leader of both the WCCA, a major affiliate in the region, and the largest squatter community threatened with removal, was welcomed into the arms of the progressive movement. The UDF turned a blind eye to Ngxobongwana's political practice in his own community. When the cold war in Old Crossroads erupted into violent confrontation between the Ngxobongwana and Memani groupings in April, and again in December, no-one in the progressive organisations, with the exception of a small group of activists in Nyanga, publicly questioned these events.[1] This would, in the long run, turn out to be a political miscalculation on the part of UDF and its affiliates, especially the WCCA and United Women's Organisation (UWO). In the future, the men who supported and fought for Ngxobongwana would just as easily turn on members of these progressive organisations. This was not apparent in 1983.

Conflict Continues Inside Old Crossroads

Less than two weeks after the Khayelitsha announcement, Old Crossroads was the scene of open and violent conflict. The fight took place between Memani and Ngxobongwana supporters. At least eight known Memani supporters were killed and scores were injured. Memani's house, shop and car were gutted in the course of the fight. It is not easy to unravel what exactly led up to or took place during the conflict which was portrayed in the media as 'tribalistic faction fights'. What does emerge from the evidence that exists is that the fight was an attempt by certain members of the Ngxobongwana Executive — with the backing of the community 'police' under Sam Ndima, and the headmen, under Jeffrey Nongwe — to establish total political and economic control over the community. For some of the leaders, Crossroads had become a place where capital was easily accumulated. Whoever controlled its political and military wing, controlled access to money. As far as Ngxobongwana was concerned, as long as Memani remained in the community he posed a threat to his own authority. The April conflict was crucial in establishing Ngxobongwana's hegemony in Old, and by corollary, New Crossroads. Although he was not in the community when the fight took place, most residents knew that Ngxobongwana's men would not have acted without his consent. This pattern of 'disappearing' on the eve of conflict situations was established with the fight of 1983.

A significant feature of the April conflict was that the men who participated as part of what was called 'Ngxobongwana's army', wore white bits of cloth to identify themselves. This was the first appearance of what would become known as 'witdoeke' in Old Crossroads. This phenomenon was not new to Cape Town. Migrants wore them during the conflict between hostel dwellers and township youth in 1976.[2] The brutality of the April killings shocked residents and the broader Cape Town public. At this time (1983) killing people with pangas and knives and, on occasion, burning them to death, was a relatively unheard of social phenomenon.

Twenty-six men were eventually arrested and brought to trial for murder and public violence. Those arrested included well known Ngxobongwana supporters — for example, Sam Ndima, Willie Soga, Jeffrey Nongwe, and Jackson Mcophololo. Of the twenty-six arrested, only four were eventually found guilty of public violence. The rest returned to Old Crossroads and to the side of Ngxobongwana.

For the remainder of the year he continued to rule and maintain his power through a combination of coercion, consent, and growing outside support. A lot of his support came from recent arrivals to Old Crossroads. A former member of the Executive Committee described why and how Ngxobongwana maintained control.

> Ngxobongwana keeps his power through promises. Most of his new members are people without rights. They will do anything . . . . He is able to find ways of getting rid of his political enemies. [He] has what I call a sense . . . [and] he is logical even though he is not well educated. [He] is like this . . . if he goes in front of a mass meeting and talks, all the people believe what he says because he has a way with words . . . . That's how he gets support. If things are going wrong in his committee he will just build up another committee. He has a good way of canvassing . . . . He plays games with the people . . . Ngxobongwana does have a gift. He can turn the sense and minds of the people . . . .[3]

For the residents, Old Crossroads had become one of the most expensive squatter communities in which one could live. Residents were unhappy with the 'taxes' collected by both Memani's and Ngxobongwana's headmen. They paid them out of fear of having their houses destroyed.[4] While economic exploitation and conflict continued inside the community, the state was putting on its own pressure. In June when KTC was cleared of squatters, and the first residents moved into fletcraft houses at Khayelitsha,[5] the state turned its attention to conflict-ridden Old Crossroads. As soon as Bezuidenhoud publicly announced that no more houses would be built at New Crossroads, it was clear that 'illegal' residents in Old Crossroads were once again under the threat of removal. At the beginning of September, Old Crossroads experienced raids for the first time since 1978. The targets of these raids were the so called 'bed people'.

Things Get Worse — Not Better

In the years when the priorities of the Old Crossroads leadership were to accumulate capital and fight over who would control the area, local community issues were not tackled. One of these issues was the growing number of residents without rights in the community. Many who found themselves in this position were lodgers who became homeless when the owners of their houses moved to New Crossroads. As soon as residents moved to New Crossroads, their shacks in Old Crossroads were demolished by Administration Board officials. Many who moved did not take their former lodgers with them. With no accommodation available to them in either New or Old Crossroads, the lodgers left behind were forced to build makeshift shelters on any available land, or in any building, in Old Crossroads. Many of the lodgers had temporary permits since Koornhof had promised that they would get houses in New Crossroads. During the survey each family was interviewed, regardless of whether they were lodgers or house-owners. In 1983, there were hundreds of homeless people 'squatting' in Old Crossroads. They were called the 'bed people' by the press.

> Most are lodgers who never got houses as they were promised.
> They were supposed to get houses, but the promises just dis-
> appeared. Nobody was following [their cases] up. Now the
> officials just raid here. They do what they want because the
> community is divided.[6]

By August there were an estimated 1000 homeless people inside Old Crossroads,[7] most of whom were sleeping on beds in the open. In the first week of September the police and Administration officials began nine consecutive raids on the 'bed people'. The raids were not passively accepted. After one of these raids women and youth in the area fought with sticks and stones. Sneeze machines were brought into Old Crossroads as riot police attempted to 'maintain law and order' in the area.[8] Brigadier Odendaal, acting Commissioner of Police, reported to the press why he felt it necessary to send in the riot police:

> During the course of the morning, the people of Crossroads
> became riotous while Administration officials were breaking
> down illegal structures . . . in order to maintain law and order
> police used tear smoke and rubber bullets . . . .[9]

Although the 'bed people' got little support from the leadership of Old Crossroads during these raids, the situation changed dramatically in late September when Dr. Morrison, the Deputy Minister of the Department of Co-operation and Development, expressed the state's position towards Crossroads:

Crossroads is a symbol of provocation and blackmail of the
government, and we want to destroy that symbolism at all
costs . . . . Crossroads will be cleared up and there must be no
doubt about that whatsoever . . . .[10]

Morrison's statement at the Cape Nationalist Party Congress was
the catalyst for a series of mass meetings in Old Crossroads to discuss
plans to move residents to Khayelitsha. After one of these meetings,
attended by several thousand Crossroads residents, the Executive
Committee called on the government to honour promises made in
1978 and 1979. The Committee said that the only way they would be
moved to Khayelitsha was if they were dead:

Dr Morrison will have to kill us first and then move our bodies
to Khayelitsha — because that is the only way we will move
there. Dr Morrison will first have to destroy the people before he
can destroy Old Crossroads . . . . The Cape Town Community
Council is burning its fingers by supporting the cruelty of Dr
Morrison. He can first move his councillors to Khayelitsha and
we would like to see his house there as well.[11]

Morrison's statement also precipitated a stronger alliance between
the UDF and Ngxobongwana. In the middle of October, the UDF and
the Executive Committee held a joint meeting at the Noxolo community hall in Old Crossroads. At the meeting, attended by thousands
of residents and members of UDF affiliates, the UDF leadership
pledged its solidarity with the community's resistance to removal.
Oscar Mpetha, UDF President of the Western Cape Region, praised
the people of Crossroads for their strength and unity. He said it
reminded him of his vow that 'if the struggle meant dying in jail, then
so be it'.[12] Ngxobongwana, who shared the platform with the UDF as
chairman of Crossroads and the WCCA, was as militant and confron-
tationist as Mpetha.

This dream will never materialize. We will resist the removal.
We will die in Crossroads . . . . If the government says black
people should go to the homelands, then why don't they go back
to Holland? It is only the black man who has no place to live.
This is our country where we were not only born but also
created. The government's dream is a false dream if they think
we will leave the Western Cape. We will not leave. We will die
here.[13]

The active alliance between UDF and the Old Crossroads leadership had begun. Those who were less trusting of Ngxobongwana, or had been targets of his economic exploitation and repression inside the community, watched from the sidelines with a certain amount of cynicism. But in 1983, Ngxobongwana was a 'popular leader' in the eyes of the leaders of most UDF affiliates. History would show that they had backed the wrong horse.

Crossroads also received support from one of its more traditional allies, the UF. Its Western Cape Regional Board convened a special meeting to respond to Morrison's statement at which it resolved to offer temporary self-help shelters to the 'bed people'. The UF also resolved to 'seek clarity on the subject of Crossroads'. Obviously still regarding Crossroads as a 'sensitive' issue, it put out a press statement reminding Koornhof of his 1979 promises to the community:

> The Minister's announcement on 5 April 1979 of a scheme for the proper housing of all members of the community complying with certain stated criteria, was according to its own terms, the product of long discussions with a view to better mutual understanding and securing the maximum of trust and co-operation . . . parts of the speech at the [Cape Nationalist Party Congress] run the risk of destroying what remains of the spirit of mutual understanding, trust and co-operation . . . . The Foundation is not oblivious of problems which have arisen but feels sure that nobody would wish to see innocent people suffering as a result . . . .[14]

While the progressive forces and the representatives of monopoly capital publicly stated their solidarity with the Crossroads struggle, residents in Old Crossroads continued to experience the harsh realities of life under the Ngxobongwana regime. 'Taxes' continued to be collected for Ngxobongwana's 'community' cars, his salary and those of a number of other local 'officials', and legal costs and bail money.[15] Residents alleged that the 'bed people' paid R10 for the right to occupy land in Old Crossroads. It was not surprising that the population of Old Crossroads was permitted to grow in leaps and bounds. Many people who came to Cape Town during the Ciskei drought easily found a home in the area.

There was mounting dissatisfaction with the amount of money residents were expected to pay to Ngxobongwana and his headmen.

Memani, who had returned to Old Crossroads in July, tried to mobilise support from amongst these disgruntled residents. In December 1983, the community was once again torn apart by violent internal conflict. In addition to bona fide Memani supporters, some targets of this latest repression were those who were refusing to pay community 'taxes'. The scope of this fight, which eventually spilled over into New Crossroads, was far greater than the one which took place in April. The fight was at no time condemned outright by progressive organisations.

The December/January Conflict

The next outbreak of violence in Crossroads began over the Christmas weekend. Ngxobongwana was, as before, away at his home in the Ciskei. The press reported that men wielding pangas, axes, and iron bars were seen roaming around Old Crossroads, 'looking for Memani supporters'. By 29 December, the area was sealed off to the public by the police. Two people were believed killed and there were reports of at least 300 people homeless in the area. The Sizamile school, symbolic for some years of the Memani supporters, was burnt to the ground. A number of homes were reported to be either demolished or burnt. According to the press, 'armed' Ngxobongwana supporters had patrolled the area for a number of days. As before, in April, they identified themselves by wearing 'witdoeke'.[16]

A number of residents interviewed at the time told the press that the fight had been sparked off by a decision of some residents to withdraw support from either side of the Executive. Residents were tired of the power struggle which had been going on between Ngxobongwana and Memani since early 1980. Memani, like Ngxobongwana, was also away on 'holiday'.

At the beginning of January, the conflict moved across to New Crossroads where a number of residents, chased from Old Crossroads, had taken refuge. Residents in New Crossroads were called to a meeting and instructed by the Working Committee — established by Ngxobongwana in New Crossroads in 1982 — to 'clean up' the area. Before too long violence erupted as Ngxobongwana's 'witdoeke' roamed the streets. They broke the windows and cut the telephone wires of suspected 'Memani supporters'.[17] Regina Ntongana and her husband Jeffrey, secretary of the Executive Committee until he had resigned following the April fights, were amongst those 'terrorised'. Both of them were in fact abducted from their daughter's house in New Crossroads where they were staying, and taken to a nearby field where they were threatened by Ngxobongwana's men. In a statement to the press from a 'safe house' in Guguletu, Regina blamed the conflict on the way 'the men' had ruled Crossroads in the last few years:

> I have been in Crossroads since 1975. We, the women, are the foundations of Crossroads. Since the men took over [in 1979], things have never been the same. The men are only concerned with their own benefits.[18]

Executive members, interviewed in Old Crossroads, told reporters that the residents — 'without force or pressure' — had decided that they wanted all Memani's supporters to leave the area. One Committee member alleged that residents had decided at a mass meeting to demolish the homes of people who did not support Ngxobongwana. He denied the 'stories' that headmen had demanded money from the community. 'Houses were demolished', he said, 'because we wanted to live in peace'.[19]

Residents in New Crossroads complained that although they had laid charges with the police, no action had been taken against the vigilantes roaming around the streets. Captain Jan Calitz, a police liaison officer for the Western Cape, told the press that the police were aware of the incidents and were investigating. 'The police', said Calitz, 'could not be omnipresent'.[20] On 16 January, thirty-one men from Old Crossroads were arrested in connection with the violence in both Old and New Crossroads.

A number of people, interviewed in Old Crossroads, told reporters that the constant fighting in Crossroads was driving people to move to Khayelitsha.

> We are being forced to go to Khayelitsha. It is not our intention, but we are running away from the fighting. It is exactly what the government wants us to do . . . .[21]

The UDF found itself in the invidious position of supporting a leadership in Old Crossroads which was accused of 'forcibly' removing residents from the area and 'driving' them to Khayelitsha. Before the UDF had a chance to make a public statement, the WCCA vice-chairman, Alfred Stuurman, issued one. In it he argued that Memani's supporters should be removed and 'go to Khayelitsha'. He also denied allegations that the WCCA chairman, Ngxobongwana, had 'sold membership cards to residents'.[22] These were given free to members, he said.

Four days later, UDF and the WCCA issued a joint statement in which they declared that they were 'not taking sides' in the conflict between the two rival 'factions' in Crossroads. Both organisations, obviously embarrassed by Stuurman's earlier statement, reaffirmed their opposition to the threatened removal to Khayelitsha. Stuurman, in fact, argued that he had been 'misquoted' in the press and that it was 'out of the question' for him to support any removals to Khayelitsha, whether directly or indirectly.[23]

In some ways the damage was already done. UDF's failure 'to take sides', or at least actively intervene to mediate in the conflict, would with time prove a fatal miscalculation. When it continued to work with, and therefore tacitly support Ngxobongwana, some residents lost faith in the progressive movement.

Notes

1. Members of TEAM (The Ecumenical Action Movement), a UDF affiliate, who lived in Nyanga East, brought out a pamphlet questioning the role of Ngxobongwana after the violence of December 1983. They were criticised heavily by leaders of the WCCA and UWO for doing this.
2. See A. Silk, op. cit., p.99.
3. Khayelitsha, Interview (1985).
4. Old Crossroads, Interview (December 1983).
5. The first residents in Khayelitsha were 200 'legal' squatters from the KTC camp. They had been living in the Nyanga beer hall with the permission of the Administration Board. Fletcraft houses are in fact nothing more than tin huts.
6. Old Crossroads, Interview No. 4 (1984).
7. *Cape Times*, 14.8.1983.
8. Ibid., 23.9.1983.
9. Ibid.
10. Ibid., 28.9.1983.
11. *Cape Herald*, 8.10.1983.
12. *Cape Times*, 16.10.1983.
13. Ibid.
14. Urban Foundation, Press Release 2.10.1983.
15. Bail money was collected from residents for those men arrested in the April fights. Ngxobongwana, for instance, had a court case pending with the Administration Board for building a brick house in Old Crossroads without their permission. Residents were expected to pay for his lawyer in the case.
16. *Cape Times*, 31.12.1983.

17. Ibid., 21.1.1984,
18. Ibid., 26.1.1984.
19. Ibid., 14.1.1984.
20. Ibid.
21. *Argus*, 27.1.1984.
22. Ibid., 17.1.1984.
23. *Cape Times*, 21.1.1984.

10 *Sand Dune squatters continue their struggle for survival in the dunes between Mahobe Drive and Old Crossroads (1982).*

11 *Inside a communal plastic 'home' — Sand Dune Squatters (1982).*

12 *KTC (1983).*

13 *Old Crossroads (1983).*

Chapter 7

Squatter Defiance – The State Rethinks

In 1983 when the state announced building Khayelitsha as a solution to the growing crisis in the Cape Peninsula, it had two major objectives. Firstly, to settle all blacks with rights to be in the Western Cape — including all those resident in Langa, Nyanga, and Guguletu — in Khayelitsha; and secondly to repatriate all 'illegal' blacks — estimated at over 100 000 — to the homelands. The state's hope was that the squatter camps would be cleared once and for all and the Cape sealed off against further influx. Like many state strategies before it, however, this Nationalist dream ground to a halt in the face of reality. Ongoing squatter resistance, together with an outright condemnation of the Khayelitsha blueprint — from a variety of quarters — would by the middle of 1984 force the state to rethink its strategies on influx control in the Western Cape. Leading local officials in the region were the first publicly to acknowledge its failure. Despite one of the most intensive periods of squatter/state confrontation in the Cape, the squatters refused to be removed. In open defiance they continued to erect plastic shelters on every available piece of land in and around the Old Crossroads squatter camp. Koornhof's attempts to tighten up influx control in the Cape had, by 1984, failed miserably. When the Cape Nationalist Party Congress met in September, there were indications that the state had shifted its policy towards the African population in the Western Cape. After weeks of 'behind the scenes politicking',[1] PW Botha sounded the death knell of the Coloured Labour Preference Policy in the Western Cape. Louis Nel, Deputy Minister of Foreign Affairs, hastened to add, however, that these concessions did not necessarily mean that 'the doors of the Cape would be opened to blacks'.[2] What he failed to acknowledge was that there were already thousands of people living 'illegally' in squatter camps who were not prepared to move. They increasingly found support from the UDF and its affiliates. Between 1983 and 1984, squatter resistance became a highly politicised issue. This was not something the state could afford.

State Repression — Squatter Resistance

In the first half of 1984 the state tried to rid the area of 'illegal' squatters by utilising repressive tactics. All the squatter camps adjacent to Old Crossroads became the targets of almost daily raids to 'flush out' 'illegal' residents. One of the hardest-hit squatter camps was a newly established one at KTC. It had come about as a direct result of the December/January conflict in Old and New Crossroads when hundreds of refugees who fled these areas set up plastic shelters on vacant land on the old KTC site. Oliver Memani, the ousted Old Crossroads vice-chairman, moved to KTC in late January, where he immediately began to try to re-establish a power base.

Timo Bezuidenhoud, released from his regular duties as Chief Commissioner at the end of March 'to do a special task',[3] proved ruthless in his handling of the KTC squatters. Not one week went by, from March until May, without a raid on the estimated 250 squatters. When it became clear that raids alone would not remove them, Bezuidenhoud tried a different strategy, offering them a piece of land next to the Nyanga Bush squatters. This was a few hundred yards from the Old Crossroads squatter camp. The KTC squatters, after considering this offer for a number of days, refused. They said that they were frightened to move to the site, arguing that 'it was better for the Board to kill us here [KTC], than for it to stand behind our brothers in [Old] Crossroads when they kill us there'.[4] Behind their statement lay a widely-held belief that in some way local officials, especially Bezuidenhoud, had sanctioned the actions of Ngxobongwana and his supporters in Old Crossroads. The state responded with more raids. These, as Bezuidenhoud publicly stated, were intended to 'persuade' Memani and his followers to move from the site. The squatters consistently refused to do so.

By July the population of the site had grown to 600. They changed their name from the KTC squatters to the 'New Crossroads' squatters as a not so subtle reminder to Koornhof and his officials that the land they occupied had been promised to Old Crossroads residents in 1979 as the second phase of the New Crossroads housing development. In an act of open defiance the squatters began painting their former Old

Crossroads house numbers on their temporary shelters.[5] They also set up an informal school and crèche. Memani built his own wood-frame shelter and informed the press that if the 'Board demolishes [my] house I will lay charges against them [because] we have been suffering too long'.[6] Open defiance continued to be met with state determination. Bezuidenhoud ordered daily raids on the KTC camp. Graham Lawrence, the WCDB's director of housing and labour, almost apologetically told a journalist from the *Financial Mail* that 'the Board had received firm orders from the Department [of Co-operation and Development] to take action [in KTC] every day'. He tried to convey something of the WCDB's dilemma: 'We do not want to act in this way — it is really not our function [to do this] as a development board'.[7] The squatters still refused to move. Memani tried to explain why this was so:

> Many of us are ill . . . . We have been left in the rain and the cold . . . . It is very important that we see Dr Koornhof face to face to tell him that we are afraid of our enemies in Crossroads . . . . We are Crossroads people and we are still wanting the Appeal Committee to investigate the cases of all 'illegals' on the waiting list . . . . If we leave we will lose all [Koornhof's] promises on Crossroads . . . .[8]

KTC was not the only area to come under attack during the first half of 1984. The Sand Dune squatters and the Cathedral Group, waiting since 1982 for their rights, as well as Nyanga Extension, all experienced raids. Bezuidenhoud accused Yamile's group of breaking their 'promises' by allowing more people to move onto their site. Hundreds of 'illegal' shelters were demolished by the WCDB during June and July. The Nyanga Bush squatters responded in the press:

> We are deeply hurt by this. If we had the power we would retaliate but [the officials] have the law on their side. I am sure God doesn't agree with these laws . . . . The authorities are playing with us. Many promises have been made to us which have not been kept. We now want to see Dr. Koornhof . . . . We have been waiting for three years for a decision about our future.[9]

The raids on both KTC and the Nyanga Bush squatters were condemned locally and abroad. Bezuidenhoud, obviously flustered by the bad publicity, assured the press that he was busy having consultations in an attempt to 'defuse' what he called a 'delicate situation'.[10] On 13 July, he announced that the Nyanga Bush squatters had been given permission to erect additional shelters on their land. Bezuidenhoud warned the squatter leaders, however, that this did not mean that new people could come into the area:

> If you see this as an opportunity to bring in additional people, then my assistance will stop.[11]

Within a matter of days, additional land was allocated to the Nyanga Bush and Nyanga Extension squatters to erect new shelters. WCDB workers laid on new water pipes, and the roads were levelled with the financial assistance of the UF who donated R10 000 for the upgrading of the area. The changed attitude towards these squatters — coming after a period in which an average of 48 homes had been demolished daily in the area — was seen by a number of people as reflecting a possible shift in thinking on influx control policies in the Western Cape. As early as March, the official estimate of the 'illegal' population in the Cape Peninsula was 60 000.[12] Before long the Chief Director of the WCDB publicly announced that the state's policy had failed miserably in the Western Cape:

> We now have proof that prosecutions are failing to stop the illegal influx and it is clearly impossible to try to stop the urbanisation process here. The only way to do this is to offer people in the rural areas what they come to seek in the urban areas.[13]

For the KTC squatters, however, the situation was not quite as simple. During August the raids were halted temporarily while Bezuidenhoud, Graham Lawrence, and Colin Appleton, regional director of the UF, tried again to persuade Memani and his followers to leave. Despite the UF's offer of a telephone at the site, and promises of police protection, the squatters once more refused the offer of the land next to Old Crossroads. Their fears were not without substance. They were based on their experiences of the fights in the area during 1983:

> Nine people have died and our houses and cars have been burnt . . . . We cannot move. How many more people must die there?

When Ngxobongwana's supporters in New Crossroads broke windows and cut telephone wires the police knew about it and nothing was done to stop them . . . .[14]

Within a few days of the rejection of the Board's offer, the raids began again. With the exception of a few individual church spokesmen, not one progressive organisation openly criticised the state's action against KTC. By saying nothing, the UDF and its affiliates tacitly supported the Ngxobongwana leadership in Old and New Crossroads, and more importantly the strategies of the state to remove the squatters.

When the continual raids failed to remove the squatters, Bezuidenhoud tried a divide and rule tactic. He asked to address the squatters at KTC and then proceeded to imply that Memani had in fact agreed to move. This had the effect of immediately fuelling tensions and divisions within the KTC camp. Memani, a long-time observer of Bezuidenhoud's methods, publicly accused him of being deliberately divisive:

At the meeting we discussed the issue [of moving to the site near Old Crossroads] as we had done several times before. But I said once again [that] this would depend on the squatters themselves. [Then] Mr Bezuidenhoud tried to [twist] my words and that started all the trouble . . . .[15]

Within a matter of days of this meeting there were reports of a breakaway group in the KTC camp. Memani, caught in the midst of ongoing conflict in the area, consistently accused the WCDB and the UDF of causing 'splits' in KTC. 'Certain groups', he said, 'were attempting to seize political control over the entire squatter community'.[16] In late November, Memani was arrested on charges of public violence and incitement to murder.[17] Although he was removed from the area this did not mean the end of the KTC squatter camp. During the next few months it mushroomed in size, along with nearby squatter camps in the Cape Peninsula. All grew in direct response to the 'July moratorium' given to the Nyanga squatters. When the Cape Nationalist Party held their Congress in September, it was apparent that they had given a lot of thought to the situation in the Western Cape.

The Beginnings of Orderly Urbanisation

The 'July moratorium' had been the first real indication that the state was finding it necessary to rethink its strategies towards urbanisation in the Western Cape. In addition to announcing publicly the failure of influx control, the Chief Director of the WCDB also made it known that the official estimate of the 'illegal' African population in the Peninsula was in the realm of 70 000-100 000. This was the highest figure ever acknowledged by the WCDB. Gunter had gone on record as saying that the population of Old Crossroads was at least 50 000, only a third of whom were believed to be 'legal' residents.[18] In September Koornhof, the master architect of the influx control strategies of the 1980s, bowed out to head the newly established President's Council. This came close to an acknowledgement that Koornhof had failed to solve any problems relating to squatting and influx control. A cabinet committee, under Chris Heunis, the Minister of Constitutional Development and Planning, was set up to reassess the position of blacks outside the homelands, as well as urbanisation.[19] At the Cape Nationalist Party Congress at the end of September, the state revealed some of its new initiatives. A number of significant resolutions were adopted:

a) to scrap the Coloured Labour Preference Policy;

b) the introduction of 99-year leasehold for Africans qualified to be in the Western Cape (Khayelitsha and 'other areas');

c) the 'repatriation' of the estimated 100 000 'illegal' Africans in Cape Town.[20]

The private sector immediately welcomed the two 'concessions' regarding 'legal' Africans in the Western Cape. Security of tenure was seen by capital as being crucial for the creation of a stable black middle class in the region. The UF had been trying to convince the state of the wisdom of this strategy from as early as 1979. 'Home ownership', as Judge Steyn of the UF had expressed it, 'may not be the way to stop riots, but it [does] achieve stability'.[21] For the first time since the 1950s, the state was moving into a position of taking co-responsibilty for the provision of housing. The kind of housing they proposed was not unlike that offered by Eiselen during the early days of apartheid rule. When the new Minister of Co-operation and

Development, Gerrit Viljoen, announced that all squatters in the Cape Peninsula, 'legal and illegal' would be resettled in Khayelitsha — 'legals' in core-houses and the 'illegals' in site and service schemes — it appeared as though the Nationalist Party had, after thirty years, come full circle.[22] This time, however, they were met with organised and defiant resistance. All the squatter leaders, including Johnson Ngxobongwana, immediately rejected the state's latest attempt to resettle them. Their resistance was openly supported by the UDF and its affiliate organisations.

The Ngxobongwana/UDF Alliance Strengthens

The UDF Western Cape Region had for some time upheld an in-principle decision to support resistance to resettlement in Khayelitsha. As early as June 1984, UDF activists had gone from door to door collecting signatures (12 000) against the removal.[23] They were still actively supporting Ngxobongwana at this time despite the fact that many former Old Crossroads residents were moving to Khayelitsha to avoid the continuing economic exploitation and repression in Old Crossroads. A former resident of Old Crossroads who moved to Khayelitsha expressed the sentiments of a growing number of people living in the area under Ngxobongwana:

> We are tired of Crossroads. People live in fear there and we are relieved to be gone. We don't like Khayelitsha and we never wanted to go, but it is the only place to run [to] . . . .[24]

Old Crossroads was increasingly being run like a mini-bantustan, with Ngxobongwana acting as 'chief' in the area. This contradictory position of his being a 'chief' and 'progressive' leader at the same time was something UDF activists and leaders seemingly ignored in their attempts to confront the state over the broader issue of Khayelitsha. The complexity of the Khayelitsha issue, given the stratification within the townships and Old and New Crossroads, was not widely appreciated within UDF circles.

Within ten days of Viljoen's announcement, the UDF Anti-Forced Removals Committee organised a solidarity meeting in Old Crossroads. Joe Marks, the UDF vice-chairperson, shared the platform with Ngxobongwana who once again won over the 'progressives' to his side with his militant rhetoric. He also used the occasion to defend himself against the growing accusation that he was exploiting residents in his community.

> You think that we are misusing your money saying lots of things behind my back but your money is in the bank . . . . Crossroads, New Crossroads and KTC is your land but Khayelitsha is not ours. [It] is for the squatters of the South African government.[25]

The WCDB, in the person of Timo Bezuidenhoud, immediately challenged this alliance between Ngxobongwana and the UDF. Known as a person not to mince his words, Bezuidenhoud publicly questioned the UDF position as regards Khayelitsha:

> If Mr Johnson Ngxobongwana, supported by the UDF, is of the opinion that he has the backing of the black masses behind him as far as Khayelitsha is concerned, he is making a grave mistake.[26]

In the South African context where political mobilisation was on the upswing in late 1984, the state could afford to take no chances. A few days later, in an attempt to win the hearts and minds of the residents, anonymous pamphlets were dropped on Old Crossroads, describing Khayelitsha as 'a beautiful township on the False Bay coast'.[27] This ideological battle between the squatter communities, supported by the UDF, and the state, continued for the rest of the year. As in the past, the state had provided divided communities with a mobilising principle to form a popular alliance. There was no doubt that Bezuidenhoud was worried. In late December, however, when violence once again erupted in the squatter camps of the Cape Peninsula, it looked as though these communities were much too divided to offer any real threat to the state. Time would show that this was not necessarily the case.

Struggles For Land and Control

In late December, the camps surrounding Old Crossroads became the scene of violent clashes. A crisis over land and resources had been developing in the area since Bezuidenhoud announced the 'moratorium' in July. The conflict, which started on the Nyanga Bush side of what

was now called the Crossroads complex, was apparently sparked off
by the issue of which squatter leader controlled what land in the
complex. Thousands of homeless people who streamed into the area
during the latter half of 1984 found themselves under the authority of
one of an estimated fifteen leaders, for each of whom squatting had
become a capital investment. The more squatters one had on the land,
the more money one could make. In nearby Old Crossroads, Ngxobongwana, who by this time considered himself the overall leader of
the Crossroads complex, closely monitored the situation.

Over the Christmas weekend, a group of squatters led by the former
chairman of Nyanga Extension, Isaac Gweliza,[28] now living in Old
Crossroads, appear to have attacked Yamile's camp. At least one resident of Nyanga Bush was reported shot and wounded during the
initial confrontation. There were press reports of 60 men, mostly
armed with sticks and clubs, wearing 'witdoeke' to identify
themselves, combing the area looking for Yamile and his group. The
conflict centred around who controlled a section of the Crossroads
complex which had mushroomed over the past three months. A large
number of the new arrivals apparently aligned themselves with
Yamile's camp.[29] Squatters from the Nyanga Bush area told reporters
that before the fighting broke out, Ngxobongwana supporters had
warned women and children through megaphones to evacuate the
Nyanga Bush and Cathedral camps, as they were going to attack the
two communities that night.

Police eventually moved into the area, firing rubber bullets and
teargas canisters to disperse the crowds who gathered. A police officer
on the scene described the task of effectively patrolling the area as
'almost impossible'.[30] 'Witdoeke' who openly gathered with sticks,
pangas, and axes on the Lansdowne Road side of the Crossroads complex, appeared to take no notice of the police.

On New Year's Eve Yamile, who had gone into hiding since the
conflict began, issued a press statement in which he openly accused
Ngxobongwana's Committee of backing the two breakaway 'factions'
which clashed with his followers over the Christmas period. These two
groups had broken away from the Nyanga Extension and Cathedral
Group squatters earlier in the year. They were led by Isaac Gweliza
and Christopher Toise. Yamile alleged that Gweliza and Toise, backed
by the Old Crossroads Executive, had attacked his community on 22
December:

I don't know why they are fighting with us. But [Old] Crossroads is definitely involved. They are keeping Mr Gweliza and Mr Toise there. Their people attack us and then they run away to Crossroads.[31]

Gweliza and Toise denied that they had started the fight. The secretary of the Executive Committee in Old Crossroads, Albert Naphakade, rejected Yamile's allegations as 'total rubbish'. As far as the Executive was concerned, he said, they didn't know who had been responsible for starting the fight — 'our only involvement is to try and settle it'.[32]

Over the New Year period the squatter leaders tried their best to settle the conflict in their area peaceably. After an all-day meeting attended by most of the squatter leaders, with the exception of Ngxobongwana as usual away in the Ciskei, the leaders agreed to instruct their supporters to 'lay down arms and stop all further violence'.[33] The meeting was attended by a number of outside organisations, including the Western Province Council of Churches (WPCC), TEAM and the WCCA. In terms of an agreement a series of mass meetings were held throughout the complex at which the squatter leaders called for peace and instructed their followers to disarm. A representative of the WCCA told the squatters at one of these meetings that internal conflict weakened their position — 'Fight apartheid not each other', he said.[34]

Although the Crossroads complex experienced increasing internal conflict over access to resources, residents were still able to overcome tensions and divisions in the face of the looming threat hanging over the area as a whole. In the course of 1985, as the threat of removal intensified, these already divided squatter communities would unite in joint resistance. When this happened the state began a major offensive to get rid of them.

Notes

1. *Cape Times*, 18.12.1984.
2. Ibid.
3. *Cape Times*, 31.3.1984.
4. Ibid., 8.5.1984.
5. Ibid., 3.7.1984.
6. Ibid., 9.7.1984.

7. *Financial Mail*, 3.8.1984.
8. *Cape Times*, 20.7.1984.
9. Ibid., 20.6.1984.
10. Ibid., 23.6.1984.
11. Ibid., 13.7.1984.
12. Ibid., 31.3.1984.
13. *Argus*, 8.8.1984.
14. Ibid., 24.7.1984.
15. *Cape Times*, 6.9.1984.
16. Ibid., 26.11.1984.
17. Ibid., 29.11.1984.
18. Ibid., 8.8.1984.
19. Ibid., 18.12. 1984.
20. Ibid., 26.9.1984.
21. *Argus*, 20.11.1979.
22. *Cape Times*, 4.10.1984.
23. Ibid., 12.6.1984.
24. Khayelitsha, Interview No. 2 (1985).
25. *Cape Times*, 22.10.1984.
26. Ibid., 24.10.1984.
27. Ibid., 27.10.1984.
28. Gweliza was deposed as chairman by the residents in September for charging them for the use of water points in the camp.
29. *Cape Times*, 31.12.1984.
30. Ibid., 27.12.1984.
31. Ibid., 31.12.1984.
32. Ibid.
33. Ibid., 5.1.1985.
34. Ibid.

Chapter 8

Caught in the Crisis

1985 witnessed a rapid escalation in the level of conflict and violence in South Africa. Many observers of the political situation inside the country date the beginnings of wide-scale violence from late 1984, when security forces moved into a number of black townships in the Vaal and Eastern Cape in an attempt to counter political mobilisation in these areas:

> The spiral of violence began in September 1984 when township-based protests signalled intensified and broad-based resistance to apartheid. The response of the security forces to the protest and resistance was immediate and severe. The heavy-handed response by the authorities was to find an echo in the militant response of township residents in the Vaal and in the Eastern Cape. By August the government had imposed a state of emergency in most of the densely populated townships in these areas. By February 1986 over a thousand persons were estimated to have died in the unrest.[1]

There was little doubt that by 1985 the South African state was faced with one of its worst political and economic crises for some decades. This was experienced at every level of the social formation. It included: economic restraints on the accumulation of capital; mounting pressure from abroad for South Africa to speed up its reform programme, promised since 1979 by P.W. Botha; and, above all, as already mentioned, the escalation of resistance inside the country's urban and rural black townships.

The State of Emergency, declared over a third of the country in July, was extended to the greater Cape Town area on 26 October. In the months between July and October, the Cape Peninsula became the scene of intensified unrest. This had started as early as January in the

14   The 'bed-people' of Old Crossroads (1983).

15   Women in Old Crossroads resist removal during the 'September raids' on the 'bed-people' (1983).

16 *Old Crossroads (1983).*

20   *Violence erupts in New Crossroads during the January 1985 rent struggle.*

21   *Militant youths confront riot police along Mahobe Drive during the February 1985 conflict.*

22 Timo Bezuidenhout (centre), Chief Commissioner of the Western Cape, following 'negotiations' with a number of squatter leaders during the February 1985 conflict.

course of a rent boycott in New Crossroads. A significant feature of the Cape Town unrest was that it started in and around the Crossroads complex. This did not go unnoticed by the local authorities. They had been aware for some time that the political Achilles heel of the Cape Peninsula lay in the 'uncontrollable' squatter camps. By 1985, they had become a major security threat to the state. The challenge to the state was now to find a way to crush resistance, as well as the support these communities enjoyed from anti-apartheid forces in the area. This did not prove an easy task, but when the State of Emergency was declared (October) possibilities increased. Less than twelve months later (May 1986), the state would have effective control over the crucible of resistance in the Cape — Crossroads.

'Ayihlawulwa Irente'— The Rent Boycott in New Crossroads

In January 1985, a rent campaign began in New Crossroads. It was largely organised by activists from CAYCO and UWO,[2] affiliate organisations of the UDF. This was the first active demonstration of UDF's presence in the area.

Since the beginning of 1982, rents had gone up R6 each year. By 1985, in the context of a deepening economic recession and broad-based political mobilisation, high rentals had become a particularly volatile political issue. Like many other black townships in South Africa where local authorities were responsible for essential services, conflict between New Crossroads residents and community councillors became endemic. General frustration and resentment centred on these representatives of the local state. New Crossroads was the first black township in the Cape Peninsula consistently to confront community councillors in their area.

In the course of one week, what had started as a peaceful protest against high rentals, led by CAYCO youth and UWO women, had become a focus of wide-scale violence and confrontation — firstly against the police, and later against so-called 'sell outs' in the community. The rent struggle in New Crossroads triggered off a chain of events with critical importance for the future.

Ngxobongwana, the recognised leader of Old and New Crossroads, and still enjoying the uncritical support of progressive organisations affiliated to the UDF, was called in to address a mass meeting in New Crossroads on 20 January. He went there, according to residents from

Old Crossroads, against the advice of a number of Executive Committee members who were unclear about the nature of the New Crossroads rent struggle. A number of them were dissatisfied that the protest was being led by CAYCO and UWO. These organisations were regarded by some residents as 'outside organisations'[3] which should therefore have a limited role in taking up Crossroads issues. This was exacerbated by the fact that activists from Guguletu and Nyanga, not from New or Old Crossroads, were seen at the forefront of the campaign. In Old Crossroads, where the Executive Committee and its allied structures, the headmen and homeguards, ruled supreme, there were not as yet branches of either of these organisations. Even the Old Crossroads WCCA zone existed only on paper. Ngxobongwana, for example, had not attended one WCCA General Council meeting since 1983. Despite these objections, Ngxobongwana addressed the rent meeting in New Crossroads. It would prove in the long term to be a fatal mistake on the part of the progressive organisations.

On the following day hundreds of women met in an open field to discuss follow-up on the rent issue. Police arrived and arrested a number of them for attending an 'illegal gathering'. Following this all hell broke loose as youths and women, many of whom were CAYCO and UWO members, roamed the area with a 'list' of so-called sell outs. In the ensuing conflict the homes of five residents were burnt, or destroyed.

In the course of the next few days, eleven people were arrested in connection with the violence and burning of property. One of them was Johnson Ngxobongwana. A UWO pamphlet, issued soon after, detailed what had led up to the arrests:

> Over 1000 people met on the field. We had nowhere else to meet. Police vans came and took two of our women. We said they must take us all and they must fetch more vans to fit us all in. 169 of us climbed into the vans. They took us to Mitchells Plain, Bishop Lavis and Pollsmoor. After we left, the police used teargas and rubber bullets on the crowd. Three people were injured and the shooting went on into the night . . . . That night the homes of five people were burnt. The people were very angry about being pushed around every day. After the burnings eleven people were arrested . . . . Mr Ngxobongwana is also in jail. Timo Bezuidenhoud has accused him and the UDF of instigating the whole business.[4]

Ngxobongwana's arrest provided youth in Old Crossroads, sympathetic to CAYCO, with the opportunity to mobilise in the area. No political organisation existed in the area at this time. There were tight controls over the youth, most of whom were organised into choirs and sports clubs. The last youth organisation to exist in the community, *Masezakhe*, was to a large extent controlled by the Executive Committee. This organisation, under the leadership of Howard Ntloko,[5] had fallen apart in the early 1980s.

Willie Soga, an Executive Committee member in Old Crossroads, held the youth 'portfolio' in 1985. Most of the youth in the area who were trying to organise a local CAYCO branch viewed him with a certain amount of distrust. But in Old Crossroads, to organise meant winning over men like Soga. One of the youths explained their problems in trying to set up a CAYCO branch:

> Soga was elected as Minister of the Youth. We had problems with Soga because he wanted Ngxobongwana to take all the decisions. We showed him the CAYCO constitution but the problem was that Crossroads itself had no constitution. So it became difficult to organise in the area. And whenever Soga attended meetings with us he would talk about making money. Soga never gave us any cultural or political education. He only came to the meetings because he wanted to discuss monies. He [also] wanted everything to be decided through him.[6]

In the midst of the rent struggle and attempts on the part of CAYCO youth to organise a branch in Old Crossroads, a new issue appeared. This was the presence of a 'removal squad' in Khayelitsha. Fears of a forced removal to Khayelitsha intensified resistance in the Crossroads complex. Unorganised youth were now at the forefront of the struggle. The state was now facing the worst crisis it had encountered in the course of its attempts to deal with the squatter communities of the Cape Peninsula.

'Asiyi eKhayelitsha' — We Are Not Moving To Khayelitsha

The arrival of a Tswana-speaking 'removal squad' in Khayelitsha in the middle of February triggered off mass hysteria in the Crossroads complex. Sam Langa, acting chairman while Ngxobongwana was in jail, called on Gerrit Viljoen to come and talk to the community:

> Dr. Viljoen thinks he can move the people of Crossroads to
> Khayelitsha like baboons on a mountain. We call on him to
> come and talk to the people of Crossroads.[7]

In Old Crossroads, where feelings had been running high following
the arrest of Ngxobongwana in January, the objective conditions were
propitious for militant resistance to a threatened removal. When the
state gave no answer but instead sent police vans into the area on
Monday, 18 February, Old Crossroads became the scene of a major
battle. By the end of the day one man had been killed and six police
vehicles damaged as violence spread from Old Crossroads to nearby
Nyanga. Ivan Toms, a doctor at the Empilisweni clinic in Old
Crossroads, told the press that many workers in the area had decided
to stay home on the Monday with their families because they feared a
forced removal:

> I spoke to Crossroads Executive Committee members this morn-
> ing and they told me there had been a community meeting last
> night at which residents decided to stay at home in view of the
> threat of removals. They did not want to leave their wives and
> children on their own in case the removals began today.[8]

By 21 February, at least eighteen people had been killed in Old
Crossroads and the surrounding areas, and over 230 people were
seriously wounded and treated at the Empilisweni (SACLA) clinic in
Old Crossroads. Most of those shot and wounded were youth. The
majority, according to the clinic staff, had been shot in the back by
either birdshot or rubber bullets.

Three days after the unrest began, Viljoen announced a number of
concessions in an attempt to defuse what was becoming a highly
embarrassing situation for the South African government. He offered
the following: 99-year leasehold for all blacks in the Western Cape;
the completion of Phase 2 at New Crossroads; and the upgrading of
Old Crossroads — Phase 3 of Koornhof's unfulfilled promises of
1979. Viljoen called on the private sector to assist the state:

> In the light of these decisions I . . . now call upon the private
> sector, employers and financial institutions to throw in their

support to make possible meaningful home ownership, and the development of facilities and infrastructure [in the black townships] . . . .[9]

The militant resistance of the Crossroads residents, together with general condemnation of police violence, locally and internationally, forced Viljoen and the state onto the defensive. Pik Botha, Minister of Foreign Affairs, promised *Newsweek* that 'important new reform initiatives which affect the people of Crossroads were in process.[10] It would be a number of months before the public became aware of exactly what these 'reform initiatives' really were. In the meantime, CAYCO-related youth in Old Crossroads used the opportunities provided by the February crisis to try once again to mobilise and organise youth in Old and New Crossroads into the organisation. Some of these youths, who by now were highly critical of the reformist nature of the Old Crossroads leadership, actively searched for possible allies to topple the power base of the Executive Committee. Their first choice was the headmen, the real power behind Ngxobongwana.

A Leadership Crisis Inside Old Crossroads

The Executive Committee, under the leadership of Sam Langa and Alfred Naphakade in Ngxobongwana's absence, had found itself ill-equipped to deal with the crisis situation developing in Old Crossroads. Soon after the conflict began, it found itself at logger-heads with the more militant youth in the community. Much of the conflict between the youth and the Executive centred around strategy and tactics. The youth wanted confrontation, not negotiation. They also felt that the Executive did not see itself as needing to be accountable to the broader community. Tensions came to a head when Bezuidenhoud, who had been desperately trying to intervene in the conflict, called Langa to his office *on his own*. Langa, on his return, was immediately confronted by a number of militant youths who accused him of being a sell out. He narrowly escaped being killed by the youth. CAYCO activists in the community intervened to protect him, and tried to convince the militant, and as yet unorganised youth, not to fight amongst themselves. Although they were also critical of Langa's action, they suspected that Bezuidenhoud had intentionally asked to meet with Langa alone.

> We tried to convince people [against] fighting with [the Executive] and rather tried to create conflict between the Executive and Bezuidenhoud . . . . What we were thinking of was 1976 when people fought with each other. We knew this [to be] a tactic of Bezuidenhoud, to create conflict [amongst us] . . . . We felt we shouldn't give him a chance by accusing people of being informers.[11]

Ngxobongwana's arrest in January had sparked off internal power struggles inside Old Crossroads. For some time headmen and homeguards in the community had been dissatisfied with the role of the Executive Committee. One of the headmen's main grievances was the way monies were being collected and administered by the Executive.

During 1984 Executive members, especially Sam Langa who was in charge of finances, had solicited a number of donations and grants from outside organisations such as the WPCC, the UF, and World Vision. These were given directly to the Executive, boosting their power inside the community, especially with Ngxobongwana. The traditional grouping inside Old Crossroads who controlled monies inside the community had, until 1984, been the local headmen. A growing antagonism towards the Executive on their part made them susceptible to an alliance with the youth who, for their own reasons, wished to overturn the Executive's power inside Old Crossroads. The more politicised youth realised, as did Ngxobongwana, that control over the community necessitated the initial support of headmen in the area. The headmen were, in 1985, as they had always been, the most powerful social force inside Old Crossroads.

> So we worked together with [the headmen] and began to attack the Executive. The headmen never realised at the time that [in doing so] they were attacking Ngxobongwana. They thought they were attacking only certain individuals. They stopped handing over monies at this time to the Executive who were then unable to pay Ngxobongwana's accounts. The Executive relied on the headmen to collect the monies [inside the community]. They never collected money themselves.[12]

This alliance between the CAYCO-related youth and the headmen sparked off a crisis of capital accumulation for the Executive and

Ngxobongwana. It also had the effect of exposing Ngxobongwana's financial situation to the broader community. Because the headmen refused to give money to the Executive, committee members were forced to explain their predicament to the residents of Old Crossroads. For the first time many residents became aware that in addition to paying Ngxobongwana's monthly salary, estimated at between R900 and R4000 per month, they were also paying for his personal expense accounts. In the period that he was away in jail the Executive Committee lost effective control over Old Crossroads to the headmen and their new found allies — the youth. By the time Ngxobongwana was released on bail in late April, the internal politics of Old Crossroads had already undergone a major transformation. Few realised at the time, however, that during his time in jail Ngxobongwana had himself radically shifted his position towards progressive organisations and the UDF. There were already hints of this change long before Ngxobongwana returned to Old Crossroads (June) following his acquittal.

During his period in jail a number of things happened which, with hindsight, make some of his closest colleagues suspect that Ngxobongwana was somehow 'bought off' during his stay in Pollsmoor prison. The first indication that 'something strange' was going on was his decision to change lawyers during February. Ngxobongwana had, until then, the same lawyer as the people arrested with him during the rental dispute in New Crossroads. Suddenly he switched lawyers and employed the services of a Pretoria-based lawyer, Isaac Swartzberg. One of his former Executive members remembers that at this time Sam Ndima, along with Willie Soga and another Old Crossroads resident, flew up to Pretoria to obtain Swartzberg's help. They did this on the explicit instructions of Ngxobongwana. Another factor which made people suspicious was that during Ngxobongwana's stay in Pollsmoor Sam Langa, the acting chairman, was one day denied access to him. Sam Ndima and Willie Soga apparently had no problems in seeing him at Pollsmoor. There were also rumours that Bezuidenhoud visited Ngxobongwana regularly during his stay in prison.[13]

In April, after more than two months in jail, Ngxobongwana was finally released on bail of R15 000 — collected from and paid for by the residents of Old and New Crossroads. Ngxobongwana's bail conditions were not usual. There were three conditions: he had to leave the magisterial district of Wynberg; he could not interfere with state witnesses or attend any public meetings; and he was allowed to stay in

King William's Town where he had to report to the police daily between 8 and 10 a.m.[14]

Ngxobongwana only returned to Old Crossroads in June when his trial began. When he did so he was confronted by the alliance between militant youth — many of them CAYCO supporters — and the headmen, under the leadership of Jeffrey Nongwe. This was something he had not anticipated, and could not tolerate. As soon as his trial ended in July, Ngxobongwana began to mobilise against CAYCO youth and progressive organisations. In doing so he was implicitly critical of the youth/headmen alliance. Timo Bezuidenhoud, in a recent court affidavit, makes special mention of the first known meeting in Old Crossroads where Ngxobongwana made public his changed attitude towards the UDF and its affiliates:

> On 14 July and after his acquittal in the Regional Court in Paarl, [Ngxobongwana] addressed a gathering at [Old] Crossroads. Here he officially declared that he is breaking his connection with the United Democratic Front and accuses this organisation of lack of support [for him] during his trial, and also that the [UDF] has caused division amongst his followers. I do not have personal knowledge of this meeting, but was informed about it and what Ngxobongwana declared on this occasion to the [UDF]. As a result of this, hostility arose between these two groups . . . .[15]

Before looking at the nature of the conflict between various groups in Old and New Crossroads, and Ngxobongwana's attempts to regain control in these areas, it is necessary to look at other dynamics within the Crossroads complex. Immediately after the February conflict between squatter residents and the SAP, Timo Bezuidenhoud had embarked on a new strategy towards the squatter communities in and around Old Crossroads. In a whirlwind round of confidential meetings with the squatter leaders during March, Bezuidenhoud worked around the clock to 'persuade' them to move to a site and service scheme at Khayelitsha — Site C. The state, personified by Timo, was, after February 1985, on the offensive.

The Art of 'Friendly Persuasion'

People trust me. You don't work with [blacks] for 37 years —

sweat with them and sometimes cry with them — without something rubbing off . . . . I want blacks to be able to develop the
sort of family life that would not only give a sense of security to
the parents, but also to the children . . . . I am a great believer
in the maxim that *a crisis creates opportunities.*[16]

On 15 March, Bezuidenhoud invited a number of the squatter
leaders, now representing at least twelve different groups, to a meeting
at his office. The meeting was attended by Mali Hoza, Melford
Yamile, Jerry Tutu, Sisa Nyandeni, and Alfred Siphika. At the
meeting Bezuidenhoud discussed the possibility of moving 'voluntarily'
to Site C. He offered the squatter groups 18 month temporary permits, provided they moved to the new resettlement area. Yamile's
Nyanga Bush community totally rejected Bezuidenhoud's offer. Their
demand remained as it had been from the beginning of their struggle
in 1981 — full rights to live and work in the Western Cape. At a mass
meeting held at Nyanga Bush, Yamile made it clear that his residents
were not prepared to discuss moving to the new township until these
rights were granted.

We do not agree to this. We want Section 10 (1) (a) rights, not
just a permit to stay for 18 months. We are not fighting. We
agree to discuss things to solve our problems but the government
is not negotiating, it is just telling us things. We've been staying
in the bush for five years with just promises . . . .[17]

Three days later two squatter leaders, Sisa Nyandeni and Mncedisi
Maqula, signed a written agreement with Bezuidenhoud saying that
they had 'voluntarily' agreed to move with their followers to Site C.[18]
The former unity of the satellite camps in resisting removal to
Khayelitsha was slowly falling apart. By 13 April, a month after
Bezuidenhoud began his discussions with the squatter leaders, six
squatter groups — including Hoza's Cathedral Group — were
reported to have signed agreements to move. Two days later, when the
first families moved to Site C, Bezuidenhoud announced in the press
that their vacated sites were 'to remain clear to facilitate upgrading
Crossroads'. This was necessary, he said, in order 'to honour the
statement of Dr. Koornhof of 5 April, 1979 to upgrade Crossroads
and establish Phase 2 of New Crossroads'.[19] On 15 April, the vacant
areas were sealed off with barbed wire. A few days later the WCDB

put up a notice next to the unoccupied land:

> You are requested to please not proceed beyond this point as this
> area is awaiting further development. [20]

Three of the largest satellite camps had, however, refused to move
to Site C. These were the 'Bez's Valley' section of Nyanga Extension
(Siphika), Nyanga Bush (Yamile), and Portland Cement (Toise).
These three leaders demanded to see Viljoen, eventually meeting with
him at the end of May. At the meeting, he refused the squatters'
demands of full residential rights. The squatter leaders, in a press con-
ference following the meeting, expressed their general sentiments
towards Viljoen:

> The Minister offers nothing new but repeats what has been said
> before — temporary rights and no security. Every Minister who
> comes along denies he has the power to change this law — when
> will there be a Minister who claims responsibility for it? [21]

By September, however, over 35 000 people were living at Site C.
Bezuidenhoud had been able to achieve in six months what, as the
Financial Mail remarked, 'many people believed impossible — the
voluntary resettlement of thousands of squatters at Khayelitsha'. [22]
The vast majority of the squatters, estimated at 70 000, still remained
behind at the Crossroads complex and KTC. As unrest escalated in the
Cape Peninsula during the latter half of the year, these areas became
flashpoints of militant resistance. This was something which local
security forces observed with growing concern.

The Ngxobongwana/UDF Alliance Crumbles

When Ngxobongwana returned to Old Crossroads in July, he initially
aligned himself with his Executive Committee in opposition to the
headmen. Although he was completely aware that he needed the latter's
support, their alliance with the youth and refusal to hand over monies
to the Executive in his absence forced Ngxobongwana to make
strategic political choices. Since he had openly come out against progressive organisations and CAYCO youth operating in Old
Crossroads, Ngxobongwana had to oppose the headmen. A CAYCO

member, living in Old Crossroads at the time, explained why he
thought Ngxobongwana turned against the headmen:

> At first Ngxobongwana heard that youth were working with the
> headmen and he didn't want political organisations in the area.
> This was the first thing that put him off working with them.
> Secondly, the headmen had stopped the money and it became
> known to the people that he was using this money to pay his
> accounts. So he was exposed. Thirdly, the headmen were very
> radical. They wanted to change everything and get rid of
> Executive members like Langa and Naphakade. Ngxobongwana
> still wanted [these Executive members] so he changed from
> working with the [headmen].[23]

When the headmen consistently refused to hand over monies to the
Executive Committee, Ngxobongwana appointed a Working Committee composed of committee members and headmen. There appears to
have been little support for the Working Committee. Ngxobongwana,
now realising that he could not regain control over the area without
the full support of the headmen, threw in his lot with them. Ngxobongwana had by now realised that the headmen had only aligned
themselves with the CAYCO youth in order to topple the Executive
Committee. As soon as both Ngxobongwana and the headmen shared
the same objectives — replacing the present Executive — a working
relationship between the two was again possible. Together they
mobilised against the Executive *and* the progressive organisations.
Sam Ndima, one of Ngxobongwana's most trusted lieutenants, was
soon at the forefront of this onslaught. He was especially critical of
unrest taking place at this time, much of which emanated from areas
in and around the satellite camps of Toise and Yamile, both of whom
welcomed the presence of youth and progressive organisations in their
areas.

Unrest in the Cape Peninsula visibly escalated following the declaration of a State of Emergency over a third of the country in July, and the
abortive Pollsmoor March which was planned to take place in August.
Each day the press reported confrontations between residents from
the 'coloured' and African townships and the security forces. The
Cape Peninsula soon resembled a war zone. Burning barricades
became a sign of the times, as did the now infamous 'necklace' — a
method used to kill people considered to be 'sell outs'. On October 26,

the state declared a State of Emergency in the Greater Cape Town area, arresting hundreds of political activists in an attempt to maintain 'law and order'. This did not, however, defuse the situation in and around the Crossroads complex. Although Old Crossroads remained remarkably 'quiet' between October and December, this was not so in the satellite camps.

In late November, while Ngxobongwana tried unsuccessfully to hold new elections[24] and close down the SACLA clinic — considered a stronghold of the progressive organisations — local security forces began to go on the offensive. In two successive 'crime-prevention' operations in early December, security forces raided the SACLA clinic and sealed off the Crossroads complex. They did so, according to their spokesmen to 'identify those involved in the recent unrest'.[25] These raids signalled the begining of a long 'hot pursuit' to flush out militant activists in these areas. On Christmas Eve, when the state announced that it had allocated R2 million for the upgrading of Old Crossroads, the objective conditions were ripe for a new alliance.

At the end of 1985, and well into 1986, there were visible signs of an active alliance between certain members of the security forces and some of the Old Crossroads leaders. Nobody could possibly have predicted then the real meaning of this for either the satellite communities or the progressive movement in the Cape Peninsula. Within six months 'witdoeke', with the uncontested support of members of the SAP and SADF, would carry out one of the most brutal and well organised forced removals ever to take place in South Africa's history. The process which led up to this is the subject of the following chapter.

Notes

1. Nicholas Haysom, *Mabangalala* (Johannesburg, 1985), p.1.
2. The Cape Youth Congress and United Women's Organisation, both of which were UDF affiliates.
3. Old Crossroads, Interview No.3, (1986).
4. 'The Struggle in New Crossroads' (UWO, 1985).
5. Ntloko was one of the delegates to Koornhof in 1979.
6. Old Crossroads, Interview No. 2 (1986).
7. *Argus*, 16.2.1985.
8. *Cape Times*, 18.2.1985.
9. Ibid., 21.2.1985.
10. Pik Botha, quoted in the *Cape Times*, 1.3.1985.
11. Old Crossroads, Interview No. 2 (1986).

12. Ibid.
13. Old Crossroads, Interview No. 4 (1986).
14. *Cape Times*, 27.4.1985.
15. Timo Bezuidenhoud, 'Affidavit', Milton Mbewana and Five others *vs* the Minister of Law and Order and Nine others, Cape Town Supreme Court (1986).
16. *Financial Mail*, 13.9.1985.
17. *Argus*, 1.4.1985.
18. *Cape Times*, 4.4.1985.
19. Ibid., 13.4.1985, 15.4.1985.
20. *Argus*, 25.4.1985.
21. *Cape Times*, 30.5.1985.
22. *Financial Mail*, 13.9.1985.
23. Old Crossroads, Interview No. 2 (1986).
24. The Working Committee approached a number of outside organisations, for example the WPCC, Black Sash, UF, and World Vision, to monitor these elections. All refused, however, because of allegations from residents and CAYCO youth that people were being asked to pay R15 to vote. After a pamphlet war inside Old Crossroads, Ngxobongwana postponed the elections until 1986.
25. See *Cape Times*, 30.11.1985, 3.12.1985.

The Battle for 'Law and Order' Begins

From the end of 1985 until the weekend of 17 May 1986 — when the brutal destruction of satellite squatter camps of the Crossroads complex and nearby KTC began — these areas, as well as New and Old Crossroads, were the focus of intense power struggles. During this five month period, political activists from progressive organisations, 'witdoeke', squatter leaders, Ngxobongwana, and the security forces were caught up in a battle for legitimate control. The conflict between 'witdoeke' and militant youth — 'comrades' — was vividly portrayed in the local media as 'black on black' violence. But the issues ran much deeper. In New Crossroads, for example, the scene of running street battles between these two groups from the end of December until mid-January, the conflict centred around how funds were raised and controlled in the community. As soon as UDF affiliates raised this issue, they began to pose a threat to the political and economic control of the New Crossroads Committee *and* that of Ngxobongwana. This committee, initially set up by him as a Working Committee in 1982,[1] operated as the New Crossroads branch of Ngxobongwana's Executive. Its methods of control were, as a result, similar. As far as Ngxobongwana and his New Crossroads officials were concerned, comrades and progressive organisations had to be destroyed. They were not the only grouping who felt this way.

For some months, local security forces, increasingly alarmed by escalating unrest in these areas, had been losing the battle for overall control. Two events in March tipped the balance of forces against the comrades. The first of these occurred when nine 'Ngxobongwana men' were killed in New Crossroads in two separate, but related, incidents. Two of the men killed were members of the New Crossroads Committee; the other seven were 'witdoeke' who had been sent into the area by Ngxobongwana to avenge the previous killings, as well as a series of attacks on the homes of Ngxobongwana supporters. The second significant event, which occurred a few days later, was the killing of two policemen in and around the Crossroads complex, one of whom was shot by a 'sniper' hidden in the Portland Cement squatter camp. From this point onwards the objectives of local security forces, the WCDB, and the Ngxobongwana leadership fused. All were determined to rid the squatter areas of militant comrades and, if necessary, destroy squatter areas supportive of them. Getting rid of the comrades, however, necessitated the complicity of the leaders from the consistently resistant satellite camps — Portland Cement, Nyanga Extension, and Nyanga Bush — all of whom were historically supportive of the progressive organisations. As a first strategy pressure was brought to bear on the leaders and residents of these communities. Between April and the middle of May, when the mass removals took place, they became the targets of intimidation, raids, and arrests by members of the security forces who consistently accused them of harbouring 'terrorists' and hiding arms in their areas. When widespread conflict broke out over the weekend of 17 May, it seemed to have come out of nowhere, taking most residents and the outside world by surprise. With hindsight, however, the signs had been there for some time. The weekend of 17 May was, in fact, merely the visible manifestation of what had been a five month war of attrition.

New Crossroads and KTC — The Battle Begins

As 1985 came to an end, reports of open conflict between 'fathers' and comrades in New Crossroads hit the local headlines. These were the terms used by the press to describe the potentially more reactionary or conservative members of the community (fathers), and the more radical residents, not all of whom were necessarily young, but most of whom showed allegiance to, or belonged to, progressive organisations. On New Year's Eve there were reports of hundreds of UDF-affiliated activists fleeing the area in fear of their lives. The conflict was allegedly sparked off by the death of a community councillor on Christmas Eve, hacked to death with pangas and set alight in his car by comrades in the area.[2] For some time before this incident occurred, however, tensions had been developing inside New Crossroads. The issue was a 'bail fund', the roots of which go back to the rent campaign of 1985 when Ngxobongwana and 169 women were arrested.

Following their arrest, the New Crossroads Committee called for a

R25 contribution from each of the 1731 households in the community. Although Ngxobongwana and the others arrested along with him were tried in June, the women's case only came up in November 1985. Three weeks after the women were acquitted, one of the committee members, Mr Benge, collected the bail money, agreeing to pay residents back on 23 December. At the meeting on that day, it turned out that the bail money was short by R6000. The residents were told to return on the 29th. The issue was not resolved on that date and the meeting was interrupted by a man called Prince Gobingca who, according to residents present at the meeting, confronted the CAYCO youth 'aggressively'. He was said to have come to the meeting accompanied by two police vans.[3] Gobingca actively mobilised vigilante groups during the next few days and on New Year's Eve was wounded when a house in which he was staying in New Crossroads was attacked with a hand grenade. In a series of 'revenge' attacks, four people were killed, and the Nomzamo crèche at KTC, used by 'maqabane [comrades] for political meetings', was burnt down. Winnie Nkosi, chairwoman of the UWO New Crossroads branch, was reported to have been abducted, taken along with two other women to Old Crossroads, and held captive in an empty container.[4] A striking feature of the conflict, according to a number of eye-witness reports, was that the police did not intervene. Gobingca, interviewed by *Cape Times* reporters on his release from Conradie Hospital a few days later, explained why he and others had found it necessary to discipline the youth:

> We must get our revenge, we cannot leave our children to play with us, we are seriously injured already. The children are being very disrespectful to the fathers . . . we are trying to get discipline into the township. If the government, [or] the police say they have any help for us, they can come and help us. *We want to find the guys who have got the grenades.*[5]

The 'fathers' of New Crossroads were not alone in their attempts to rid the area of comrades. In Old Crossroads, after Sam Ndima ordered the release of Winnie Nkosi and two other women from an informal 'jail' in the area,[6] he too threatened the comrades:

> Mrs Nkosi and the others were helping the comrades to cause trouble and to fight the fathers. The fathers wanted to punish

17   Chairman of Old and New Crossroads, Johnson Ngxobongwana, poses
with two community cars bought for him in 1983.

18   'Witdoeke' emerge in the course of conflict in Old Crossroads in April
and December 1983.

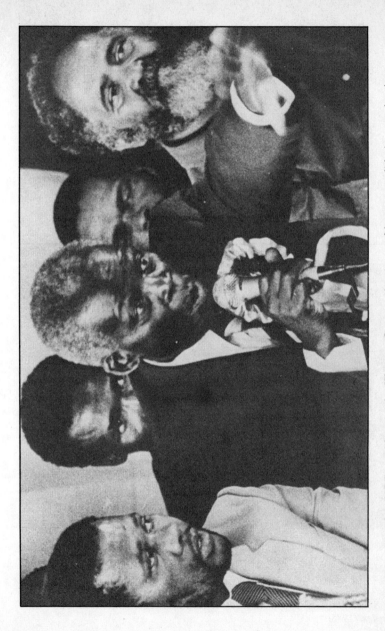

19 Oscar Mpetha, UDF president in the Western Cape at the time, addresses a solidarity meeting in Old Crossroads (1984).

23   *SADF 'buffels' patrol Lansdowne Road, alongside the Crossroad complex (1985).*

24   *Burning barricades on the Cape Flats (1985).*

25 *Women from New Crossroads demonstrate against Johnson Ngxobongwana (1986).*

them for a while . . . . Unless the maqabane cool down the people of Old Crossroads will hunt them down and beat them again. I released the people, but they must be careful. The maqabane have to stop making petrol bombs and holding 'Kangaroo courts'. We will not allow them to beat and punish their own people.[7]

Ndima was expressing the sentiments of many residents in the townships and surrounding squatter camps when he talked of 'Kangaroo courts' and the punishment of black people by certain comrades. The intimidatory methods used by militant youths in enforcing a consumer boycott and Black Christmas during the last months of 1985 had, in fact, created the potential for mobilising reactionary forces against comrades and residents in some way aligned with these campaigns. During these campaigns, organised in the last half of 1985 by a variety of UDF affiliates, militant youths from the black townships often ruthlessly dealt with residents suspected of not supporting the campaigns. There were, for example, numerous reports of militant youths forcing residents to drink fish oil, or swallow washing powder, as punishment for not following the 'correct line'. The actions of these 'comrades' alienated a large percentage of residents from the townships and surrounding squatter camps. In the next few months the Ngxobongwana leadership and the security forces would take full advantage of, and exploit, these grievances.

Old Crossroads and Ngxobongwana

Ngxobongwana had, since his return to Old Crossroads in July 1985, tried to legitimate his rule over New and Old Crossroads. This, as we have seen earlier, had been thwarted by opposition from CAYCO youth in both areas. After the seemingly successful ousting of progressive organisations and activists from Old Crossroads during December and January, the way appeared clear for him to carry out his elections. According to Executive members reasonably close to him at the time, Ngxobongwana wanted to legitimate his power for a number of reasons. He badly wanted control over the promised upgrading of Old Crossroads and the R2 million promised for the scheme by Chris Heunis. In order to be accepted as a legitimate leader by the state, Ngxobongwana had to formalise his authority over New and Old Crossroads. The only way he could do this was to join hands with black local authorities. During January, Ngxobongwana was seen having a number of meetings with known community councillors from Langa and Guguletu. As a result of this, some of his most loyal Executive members refused to participate in the upcoming elections.[8]

Despite this dissatisfaction, Ngxobongwana, with the support of a newly constituted Working Committee, held elections on 24 February. Although he was re-elected as chairman of New and Old Crossroads, the vast majority of residents in these areas did not cast a vote. Less than 6000 out of an estimated population of over 80 000 took part in the elections. The suspicions of some of his former Executive members proved well founded when, at a community meeting held at the beginning of March, Ngxobongwana publicised a letter he had sent to Chris Heunis. In it were expressed a number of the new committee's wishes. One was for the speedy implementation of the Crossroads upgrading scheme. The other was the formalisation and acceptance of the committee by Heunis's department. It is worth quoting:

Dear Sir,

In the first instance on behalf of the Crossroads community we wish you all the compliments of the year 1986 and all successful deliberations at all your parliamentary sessions.

Sir, after the public announcement about the upgrading of Crossroads and the setting aside by the government of the sum of 2 million rands for the same, we people of Crossroads made a unanimous decision of electing a committee by a secrete [sic] ballot, a committee which will form a link between us as a community and the Urban Foundation and your Planning and Development Department.

Our election started on the 24:02:1986 and closed on the 28:02:1986. The results brought out the following as successful men out of 27 candidates.

Mr J. Ngxobongwana	3 629	votes
Mr S. Langa	522	"
Mr E.Z. Ndzungu	370	"
Mr Mdloyi	286	"
Mr A. Mbiza	275	"
Mr E. Khedama	168	"

| Mr Mzilikazi | 217 | " |
| Mr P. Mzaca | 116 | " |

The Executive has added 4 others to form a committee of 12.[9]

In addition to a number of requests for certain community facilities, the letter made it clear that the upgrading scheme could not proceed unless the surrounding squatter camps in the Crossroads complex were somehow cleared of their existing residents:

> Honourable Minister, as Crossroads has many dwellers we anticipate a difficulty in the upgrading of Crossroads though if it was done long ago there would be no difficulty. Crossroads during the years we were told about [the] 1st and 2nd Phase had vacant ground where levelling could be started for the first buildings. The Chief Commissioner now happened to bring people from Hout Bay, Killarney and put them even on rugby and soccer fields. All in all sir, I want to report to you that the Crossroads community is looking forward to this upgrading which of course is long overdue.[10]

There can be little doubt, as the content of this letter shows, that Ngxobongwana was setting himself up to become a local black authority in Old and New Crossroads. He also wanted all the surrounding land, from Old Crossroads to KTC, for the new upgrading scheme. But this necessitated the removal of the communities occupying the land.

As early as December 1985, squatter leaders from the surrounding satellite camps had received veiled threats from Ngxobongwana. After a meeting attended by Hoza, Siphika and Toise, at which Sam Ndima told the leaders to 'get rid of comrades' living in their communities, Toise met Ngxobongwana in Sam Langa's house in Old Crossroads. According to Toise, Ngxobongwana had jokingly told him that he wanted Portland Cement cleared by 1986. Toise did not take Ngxobongwana's comment seriously at the time. It was only some time later, according to Toise, that he realised that Ngxobongwana meant what he had said.[11]

Turning Points

Ngxobongwana's power was once again threatened by events taking place at New Crossroads, where the struggle over the 'bail fund' remained unresolved. The 'bail fund' symbolised the continual contestation between UDF affiliates and the New Crossroads Committee for legitimate rule in the area. On Tuesday 18 March, two young women whose families had refused to contribute to the fund were allegedly attacked with an axe by 'Ngxobongwana men'. Following a mass meeting the next night in New Crossroads, attended mostly by women and youth, the house of one of the men who attacked the young women was burnt down. Others, belonging to residents considered to be 'sell outs' were also destroyed. Later in the day, the police revealed that the bodies of two New Crossroads Committee members, James Mehlala and Fenfolo Sitwaye, were found hacked to death in the early hours of the morning.[12] Ngxobongwana and Sam Ndima did not take long to respond.

On the evening of 20 March, about 300 armed 'witdoeke' moved into New Crossroads to 'fetch the belongings' of residents of New Crossroads, driven from there during the week. They were met by hundreds of residents from New Crossroads and nearby Nyanga who had been tipped off about the revenge attack. In the ensuing battle between 'witdoeke' and residents, 7 'witdoeke' were killed. In the space of 48 hours, 9 of Ngxobongwana's men had lost their lives.[13] A 'witdoek' hostage, Nkosana Mdini, captured by comrades in the area on the night of the fighting, spilled the beans in an exclusive interview to the *Cape Times*.

> After work on Thursday, Sam Ndima went around with a loudspeaker and called on all the men my age and younger to bring their weapons and go to Mr Ngxobongwana's office. He said that anybody who didn't go would be killed or burnt in his shanty. Some of the men had guns.[14]

According to Mdini, the men were told to wear white cloths on their heads and legs 'so we could know each other'. Ngxobongwana then told the men that they were to go to New Crossroads 'to fetch the belongings' of former residents recently kicked out of the area by activists from the progressive organisations. Ngxobongwana drove beside the men along Lansdowne Road until they came to the entrance of New Crossroads. There they were met by two police vehicles which escorted the 'witdoeke' into the area. Ngxobongwana stayed behind. Soon after this the 'witdoeke' were confronted by angry residents from the

community. Mdini alleged that this kind of attack had been organised
in the past by Ndima and Ngxobongwana. 'People have been com-
manded on several occasions to go and attack', he said.[15] CAYCO,
UWCO, and the WCCA, of which Ngxobongwana was still the official
chairperson, issued a joint statement condemning the action:

> Mr Ngxobongwana, through his actions, has brought grief to the
> families of these seven men who died away from their homes. He
> is using their ignorance for his own political purposes and we
> strongly regret any injuries or deaths which may have been
> suffered. Our people must resist being made cannon fodder by
> people like Mr Ngxobongwana. We have to defend our lives and
> property against these attacks and nobody can be held responsible
> for the seven deaths — it was a war of resistance waged by the
> whole community, fathers, mothers and the youth.[16]

Shortly after this event Ngxobongwana 'disappeared' from Old
Crossroads, leaving the community under the charge of his trusted
lieutenant, Sam Ndima. Old Crossroads residents were left divided between those who were bent on revenge, and others who were angry at
Ngxobongwana for the loss of what they considered innocent lives. For
the next two months Ndima and his men would actively mobilise to rid
the surrounding areas of comrades once and for all. Their interests were
beginning more and more to coincide with another group who had for
some time been monitoring the squatter camps and surrounding
townships with some concern. This was the repressive arm of the state
— the security forces.

Within a few days of the deaths of these seven 'witdoeke', two
policemen died in the Crossroads complex. One of them, Constable
Patrick Legong, was, according to rumour, shot in the head by a
'sniper' from the Portland Cement squatter camp, using an AK-47.[17]
After this event the security forces went on a major offensive in the
Crossroads complex. As far as they were concerned, the situation in the
black townships and squatter camps had been deteriorating for some
weeks before this incident took place.

On 3 March, 7 alleged ANC 'terrorists' were gunned down by police
in a shoot-out in broad daylight in NY 1, Guguletu. At their funeral on
the 15th, ANC flags were paraded in open defiance of a magisterial
order banning any political content at the funeral. A reported 30 000
township residents, mostly women and youth, attended the funeral.[18]

These events were followed in quick succession by the killings in New Crossroads and the deaths of the two policemen. After the shooting of Legong, the security force presence in the black townships and surrounding squatter camps visibly intensified. For the first time a paratroop unit, apparently stationed in the Cape Peninsula for some time, was deployed.[19]

The main targets of the security forces, however, appeared to be the satellite camps. In the period immediately following this attack on the police, they became the targets of massive daily manhunts for ANC 'terrorists' and possible arms caches. The squatter leaders were the first to come under pressure. Six days after the deaths of the policemen, Melford Yamile, leader of the Nyanga Bush squatter camp, was detained along with ten other residents from his area, and held under Section 29 of the Internal Security Act.[20] Christopher Toise and Alfred Siphika, the leaders of Portland Cement and Nyanga Extension, were both arrested in the weeks to follow. Toise, who had his home searched for 'arms' at least six times between March and May, was consistently hounded by members of the security forces who believed that the 'sniper' was hidden inside his community.[21] Substantial evidence exists that Sam Ndima and his followers in Old Crossroads assisted the security police in their 'investigations'.[22]

Ndima And His Followers On The Offensive

As has been shown, Ndima and Ngxobongwana had been threatening leaders from the satellite camps since December 1985. This continued into 1986, and extended to committee members inside Old Crossroads believed to be sympathetic to comrades and the progressive organisations. As early as January a number of these men were intimidated by Ndima and Nongwe, leader of the headmen, and as a result fled Old Crossroads seeking refuge in Yamile's camp nearby.[23] After the March killings in New Crossroads, Ndima actively sought assistance from the police to rid the area of both the comrades and the surrounding satellite camps. Col. Hugo Schreuder, District Commander at Athlone, submitted an affidavit to the court during the KTC interdict hearing[24] in which he reported that Ndima and a number of his followers had on several occasions during March and April visited his offices, asking for assistance against attacks on his people by the comrades. According to Schreuder, a formal meeting was arranged

between him, Ndima, Prince Gobingca and a number of others at
Athlone on 24 April. At this meeting, where Ndima asked the police
for guns, Schreuder says he explained to him that guns could only be
lawfully acquired.[25] Be that as it may, Ndima had already indicated to
the residents of Old Crossroads that he had been promised guns by the
police.

According to Simon Mngakane, a former resident of Old Crossroads, Ndima had first told them about this at a meeting which took
place at the Noxolo community hall on 13 April.

[On the night of] 13 April 1986, a general meeting of Crossroads
residents was called . . . by Sam Ndima . . . . [He] told us that
he had been given firearms by the station commander of the
South African Police at Athlone. He said [these] would be given
to the headmen and to the community police of Crossroads. He
explained that these weapons were going to be used against [men
from] the old committee who had resigned . . . and against the
comrades [who] he said were a bad influence in Crossroads.

At this meeting I stood up and asked Ndima since when had
he [become] a leader of the Crossroads people. [He] said that it
had nothing to do with me. I was already unpopular with
Ndima. [In March when he] had called all the men of Old
Crossroads to fight I refused . . . . [After this meeting] he took
the number of my house.[26]

The next round of significant events occurred on and around 29
April. Ndima invited the leaders of Nyanga Bush, Portland Cement,
and Nyanga Extension to a meeting which he held at Hoza's camp in
Site C. Only Siphika attended, although members of Yamile's and
Toise's committees were present. At the meeting Ndima threatened to
'flatten' all the satellite camps, including KTC. As Siphika put it in an
affidavit,

On 29 April I attended a meeting called by Sam Ndima . . . [his]
Committee was obviously also there. [Ndima] informed us that
he had been promised 200 guns for himself and 200 for Mr
Hoza, the leader of the Site C squatter group. [He said that
these] guns would be used to flatten all the squatter camps at
Portland Cement, Nyanga Bush and Nyanga Extension. The
reason for this was [he said] because we had too many 'comrades'
in our squatter camps.[27]

On the night of the 29th, former Old Crossroads Executive members and Toise were harassed by Ndima's men as well as members of the security forces. Albert Naphakade, for example, who had resigned from the Executive in January, had his house demolished that night; and Elliot Dyakophu, formerly one of Ngxobogwana's closest allies, woke up when stones were thrown at his house.[28] Toise had his house shot at and a teargas canister thrown inside it at 3 a.m. on 29 April.

> At about 3 a.m . . . . I was woken up by several shots. I dived under my bed and I could see through the curtain separating my bedroom and my lounge that there was a fire burning . . . I could hear all the women [who were holding a prayer meeting for me before my court case in the morning] and my wife screaming with terror in one of the rooms. I then heard several shots striking the corrugated iron walls of my shack . . . . I then saw the door being kicked down and several policemen entered . . . . All of [them] were in plainclothes . . . . I recognised some of them [because of my previous arrests and interrogation] . . . . I and the women who were hiding in my house were then herded outside of the house and the women were told to stand behind [it] . . . . I was then surrounded by a group of policemen who pointed their guns at me and who asked me several threatening questions about the whererabouts of arms and weapons . . . . Shortly [after this] the policemen left . . . . After that attack neither I nor my wife stayed in our house for fear of again being raided and attacked by the police . . . .[29]

As we have seen from the detention and arrests of Yamile, Toise and Siphika, from the end of March the security police had constantly been harassing these leaders and residents in their communities, searching for 'arms' and weapons. Continuing unrest along the Klipfontein Road and Lansdowne Road sides of the Crossroads complex in late April kept the security forces continually busy in the area.[30] At the beginning of May, the real build-up to the May-June removals began.

Pressure Mounts in the Crossroads Complex

On 1 May the Crossroads complex was effectively sealed off. Massive 15-ton concrete blocks, 15 cm thick and 10 metres long, were placed

across all the major access points. One was placed at the Crossroads
entrance on Old Klipfontein Road; another at Stock Road and
Lansdowne Road; and five others at the intersection of Lansdowne
Road and New Eisleben Road. Delivery vehicles and press were told
that if they entered these areas, or the surrounding black townships, it
would be 'at their own risk'.[31] Louis Le Grange announced a day later
that police curbs on funerals in the Western Cape, and around the
country, would be strictly enforced.

> These conditions are not unenforceable and they will be en-
> forced by the security forces. *We have now had enough* [my
> emphasis].[32]

Inside Old Crossroads the pressure was also mounting. On Thurs-
day 1 May, Sam Ndima, accompanied by members of the SAP, searched
Dyakophu's house looking for guns which they said belonged to Toise
and Yamile. By this time Ndima was openly walking around Old
Crossroads in the company of members of the security forces. He was
also, according to Dyakophu's evidence, very soon seen to be carrying
guns, as were other members of the Executive and homeguards.

> On Thursday, 1 May 1986, at dawn, Mr Ndima accompanied by
> the police came to my house to search for weapons allegedly
> belonging to Toise and Yamile . . . . I was struck by the fact
> that Ndima had such easy access to the police . . . . Later [that
> evening] Ndima held a meeting at Noxolo School . . . . I was
> present at the meeting . . . . Ndima told the gathering that he
> was going to get guns from the police . . . . [He] asked how
> many Crossroads [homeguards] there were and said that they
> would all be given guns . . . . [A few days after this] we saw
> followers of Ndima openly carrying guns. I myself saw Ndima
> . . . and various members of the Crossroads police armed.[33]

On Sunday 5 May, a grenade was thrown at Ngxobongwana's
house.[34] He was not in the house as he was still 'in hiding'. This
triggered off a major onslaught against former Executive members
and anyone else suspected of being in any way related to this attack.
After a mass meeting at Noxolo on Sunday evening, Ngxobongwana's
followers, led by Ndima and Gobingca, mounted a counter-attack. On
the following morning they took the keys from the SACLA clinic and

closed it down. Executive members had for some time been unhappy with the 'politics' of certain clinic staff. They gave a number of reasons for closing down the clinic: the fact that CAYCO held meetings there; rudeness of the staff to patients; the SACLA printing press only printed for CAYCO; and that particular members of staff, involved in progressive organisations, were openly critical of the Executive Committee.[35] Following this, Ndima and his men went on a witchhunt for possible CAYCO members and anyone they suspected of being sympathetic to the comrades. The press, the Black Sash, and the Progressive Federal Party (PFP) Unrest Monitoring Group became inundated with frantic calls from Old Crossroads residents who were being physically driven out of the community. Jan Van Eck, MPC for Groote Schuur at the time, commented in the press on the build-up of tension in the area:

> It's quite clear that tensions are building up. I am appalled by the general state of anarchy in the area. There's a general atmosphere of total instability.[36]

In the course of the next few days, all the former Executive members known to be openly critical of Ngxobongwana and Ndima were routed out of Old Crossroads. Most of them moved in with relatives and friends in New Crossroads. From here they tried to mobilise support to topple the existing power structures inside Old Crossroads. But it was already too late. On Friday evening, 16 May, residents in the Crossroads complex heard what they thought were 'routine' shots coming from police patrolling the area.[37] Few realised that this was the beginning of a massive onslaught against the satellite camps. Five days later the only thing that remained of Nyanga Bush, Nyanga Extension, and Portland Cement were the people's memories. During the next four weeks these areas, as well as KTC, would become operational war zones.

Notes

1. Ngxobongwana set up this committee in 1982 during the period that he feared a takeover of both New and Old Crossroads by Memani and his supporters. It became formalised over the years into the New Crossroads Committee, but was never democratically elected by residents in the community. This committee acted as the New Crossroads wing of the Executive Committee in Old Crossroads, directly accountable to Ngxobongwana.

2. *Cape Times*, 1.1.1986.
3. N. Haysom, op. cit., p.112.
4. *Argus*, 2.1.1986.
5. *Cape Times*, 3.1.1986.
6. Since 1983, homeguards in Old Crossroads had used a building on the edges of the community, the Crossroads Development Centre, as a jail. Residents, charged with a variety of petty crimes, were kept there for whatever length of time the homeguards thought fitted the crime. The Catholic Church, owners of the building, constantly fought with Ngxobongwana about the way this building was being used.
7. *Cape Times*, 7.1.1986.
8. Old Crossroads, Interview No. 4 (1986).
9. Letter from the Crossroads Committee to Chris Heunis, Minister of Constitutional Development and Planning, dated 5.3.1986.
10. Ibid.
11. C.Toise, Interview (1986).
12. *Cape Times*, 20.3.1986, 21.3.1986.
13. Ibid., 22.3.1986.
14. Ibid., 26.3.1986.
15. Ibid.
16. Ibid.
17. Ibid.
18. Ibid., 17.3.1986.
19. Ibid., 28.3.1986.
20. Ibid., 5.4.1986.
21. C. Toise, op. cit.
22. Ibid.
23. See Affidavit, Wellington Mzawupheli Qobo, filed as evidence in the case of Milton Mbewana and Five Others *vs* The Minister of Law and Order and Ten Others, op. cit. (All affidavits subsequently referred to were filed as evidence in the KTC interdict. They will therefore be cited simply as Affidavit).
24. This interdict was brought against the Minister of Law and Order, the Minister of Defence, and the head of the SAP, General Coetzee, by residents from Portland Cement, Nyanga Extension, Nyanga Bush, and KTC in the aftermath of the destruction of the satellite camps in May.
25. Col H. Schreuder, Affidavit.
26. Simon Mngakane, Affidavit.
27. Alfred Siphika, Affidavit.
28. See Albert Naphakade and Elliot Dyakophu, Affidavits, op. cit.
29. C. Toise, Affidavit.
30. See *Cape Times*, 29.4.1986 for accounts of unrest.
31. *Argus*, 1.5.1986.
32. *Cape Times*, 2.5.1986.
33. E. Dyakophu, Affidavit.
34. *Cape Times*, 5.5.1986.
35. Ibid., 7.5.1986.
36. Ibid.
37. Simour Menziwa, Affidavit.

Chapter 10

The Destruction of the Satellite Camps and KTC

During the period 17 May to 12 June 1986, Cape Town and the international community witnessed the most brutal destruction and forced removal of squatter communities in this country's history. In a period of less than four weeks, an estimated 70 000 squatters from Portland Cement, Nyanga Bush, Nyanga Extension, and nearby KTC became refugees in their own land as hundreds of 'witdoeke' with the uncontested support of members of the security forces declared war on these communities. Countless sworn affidavits from the residents of these areas, reporters, clergymen, and other eyewitnesses, bear testimony to the fact that this was not spontaneous. From the evidence, it appears that the systematic destruction of these squatter communities took place in two separate, but related, operations which were carefully planned and executed with military precision.

Since the beginning of 1985 these squatter camps had become a focal point of organised resistance to the South African state. This resistance pulsed to the rhythm of a more generalised level of protest in the country. By the end of the year, the state found itself forced to extend the State of Emergency — declared in July — to the Western Cape. From the end of 1985 until the destruction of these camps in mid-1986, militant activists from progressive organisations, as well as residents of squatter communities supportive of them, came under increasing pressure from the security forces. This, as we have seen, intensified during April and early May 1986, when members of the security forces, often assisted by leaders from Old Crossroads and their supporters, consistently raided these camps searching for 'terrorists' and suspected arms caches. When these camps were eventually razed to the ground, three specific groups gained from their destruction — the leadership of Old Crossroads, eager for more land and control; local state officials who had been trying unsuccessfully for three years to get the squatters to move to Khayelitsha; and, above all, local security forces.

Those who lost this battle for control were not only the more militant squatter leaders but, and perhaps more significantly, anti-apartheid organisations who now found their supporters scattered and potential power bases destroyed. In the aftermath of what was essentially a major political and military defeat, these groups faced the arduous task of trying to reorganise, not only to survive, but also to continue the struggle for rights and freedom in the context of yet another State of Emergency.

The Destruction of Portland Cement, Nyanga Bush and Nyanga Extension

The general public first became aware of the battle raging in the Crossroads complex on the morning of 19 May. Newspapers carried vivid reports and photographs of houses burning and residents fleeing the area as militant 'witdoeke' went on the attack. Police, who were reported to be on the scene, seemingly did very little to intervene.

> Warring factions from three squatter camps fought in Lansdowne Road, flinging stones and petrol bombs and exchanging shots as scores of squatter shacks blazed in the background, leaving thousands homeless . . . reporters saw Casspirs standing by without apparently intervening — an accusation which has been emphatically denied by the police . . . .[1]

The fighting, which would continue for six days, had begun between 6 p.m. and midnight on Saturday the 17th, when residents of these camps first heard gunshots. The first community to be physically attacked was Portland Cement. As early as midnight Selina Valo saw houses burning in her community.

> At approximately midnight on Saturday 17 May I looked through my window and witnessed the burning of five houses near my home at Portland Cement . . . . The people I [saw] starting the fire were two white soldiers, one in a red tracksuit top, and one in a blue and white tracksuit top . . . . [O]thers were Khethelo, a man who formerly belonged to Mr Toise's

LAW AND
ORDER!

Afrapix

Afrapix

26 'Witdoeke' on the offensive (May 1986).

27 Lansdowne Road, alongside burning Portland Cement squatter camp
(May 1986).

28   Young 'comrades' fleeing from teargas and 'witdoeke' (May 1986).

29 Women pray outside the houses of parliament after the devastation of their homes (May 1986).

30 A former resident, now a refugee, reflects the human suffering which followed the destruction of the satellite communities.

31 *Security forces on patrol between the burnt-out camps and Old Crossroads (May 1986).*

[Committee] but who has [now] joined the Crossroads' vigilantes . . . Nevana, Dana, Kili, and one other black person. I saw Khethelo throw a piece of burning tyre onto the roof of one of the houses nearby [causing it] to catch fire. I [don't] know for certain how the other houses [were burnt] but thought that flames from the first house could have spread to the others. I took some of my clothes and took refuge behind Mr Toise's house. On Sunday I fetched more things from my home which was then burnt down by the Crossroads vigilantes . . . .[2]

There were countless reports of white men wearing balaclavas, together with 'witdoeke', roaming around Portland Cement in the early hours of Sunday morning, attacking residents and setting the houses on fire. By 5 a.m. the whole of Portland Cement was ablaze. Lansdowne Road was lined with hundreds of former residents standing helplessly alongside possessions salvaged from the embattled area. Others, whose houses were not yet burnt, tried desperately to stop the attack. According to residents, the police, who were in the vicinity, did nothing to assist the residents of Portland Cement.

On my way to my brother's shack I found a large group of Portland Cement residents standing outside. They were looking towards the [area] between Old Crossroads and Portland Cement where a group of 'witdoeke' were standing. [They] were shouting to the residents that they must move out of the area. The 'witdoeke' then started shooting and throwing stones at the residents of Portland Cement. [These residents], with me amongst them, ran towards Lansdowne Road. Two Casspirs which had been parked more or less at the corner of Lansdowne Road and the boundary between Old Crossroads and Portland Cement then drove away [from where they were standing] and [the people] inside of the Casspirs opened fire on us . . . . ['Witdoeke'] from Old Crossroads then advanced and started to burn the shacks systematically from those nearest to Lansdowne Road . . . to those deeper inside Portland Cement . . . .[3]

While Portland Cement was still burning, the attackers moved towards their next target — Nyanga Bush. 'Witdoeke' had apparently started mobilising for this in the early hours of the morning. At 8 a.m. residents from the area, who had been watching the chaos in nearby

Portland Cement, saw Sam Ndima standing on a hill, not far from Nyanga Bush. He was calling Crossroads men, asking them 'to bring anything that could be used as a weapon to Noxolo School'.[4] From 11 a.m. on Sunday, continuing into Monday, Nyanga Bush was brutally destroyed by Ndima and his 'witdoeke'. Although residents tried their best to salvage their belongings and, especially on Monday, beat back the 'witdoeke', police assistance to the 'witdoeke' made this impossible.

> At about 11 a.m. the vigilantes [came] to my camp. [They] burnt three houses. While this took place the police [who were there at the time] did nothing. In fact, when I and a group of over 200 men [tried] to resist the attack of the vigilantes [they] ran and stood together with the police at the Casspirs. The police then fired [about] five shots [which forced] my group to run towards Nyanga Extension. I then returned with a group of about 400 men, women, and children to Nyanga Bush. My intention was to stop [them] from burning our houses. When the vigilantes saw [us] approaching they ran towards the Casspirs again. They then waited with the police. We went towards the Casspirs [but] the vigilantes who were armed with rifles, as well as the police, opened fire on us. They fired more than 20 shots at us. We then ran towards Nyanga Extension. [Another] group of vigilantes, about 600, then joined [the other] group at Nyanga Bush. They [then started] to burn about 30 to 35 houses. The four Casspirs were then joined by four more Casspirs. The vigilantes moved [freely] amongst the Casspirs. The police at no stage attempted to stop the vigilantes from burning our houses. They continued [with the burning] until 7pm. [They] had by this time burnt about 200 houses . . . . I and all the residents of Nyanga Bush then returned to try and put out some of the fires. The police had not withdrawn and [when] we attempted to get back to our houses they fired at us, even the women. The vigilantes [came back] at around 10 p.m. Their numbers had now grown to [over] a 1000 men. [They] started to fire at us . . . . [So did] the police who had not left the area. Many shots were fired at us. I then left with my group to go to Nyanga East . . . .[5]

While some 'witdoeke' were busy burning Nyanga Bush others, allegedly accompanied by the police, began the third and last prong of this paramilitary operation. This time the target was Nyanga

Extension. Alfred Siphika, the leader of this camp, witnessed the burning of his community.

> We saw that the fighting had extended to Nyanga Bush which was between us and Portland Cement . . . . I decided to go and investigate [and] saw two Casspirs encircling the squatter camp. People were fleeing from Nyanga Bush trying to gather their belongings and the police, instead of assisting them, were shooting at them. At this [time] I decided to retreat. I ran to Mahobe Drive. From [there] . . . I saw a Casspir go from Nyanga Bush . . . into Nyanga Extension . . . and soon [afterwards] the houses started burning. I [stayed] at Mahobe Drive all day [watching] the situation. From time to time we tried to get back to Nyanga Extension to [fetch] our belongings but each time we [tried] to we were shot at by the police and 'witdoeke'. Eventually when all of our houses were burnt down [and] we realised that [there was nothing we could do] about it . . . we left Mahobe Drive. I went to KTC . . . .[6]

The pattern of events which these former residents describe continued through the night into Monday. By this time, however, scores of township residents, especially those who lived along, or nearby, Mahobe Drive — separating the Crossroads complex from Nyanga East — had joined refugee squatters in running battles with 'witdoeke' and police. For most of Monday this area resembled a war zone. Militant youths, some of whom reportedly carried handguns and AK-47s, tried repeatedly to beat back the constantly approaching 'witdoeke'.[7] By the end of the day, the outcome of this battle was, to say the least, devastating — at least 13 people were dead; 75 injured; an estimated 20 000 squatters were homeless; and approximately two-thirds of the houses in the area (2000) had been burnt.[8] In the midst of the chaos and confusion, relief agencies tried desperately to aid the battle-scarred victims. First aid posts, tents, and soup kitchens were set up at Zolani Centre in Nyanga East, and along Lansdowne Road, for the thousands of homeless refugees. These agencies stretched themselves to the limit to meet the needs of the bewildered men, women, and children of the destroyed satellite camps. A Red Cross spokesperson on the spot summed up the essence of the situation:

> It's just impossible to work out how many people need our help. It's chaos out there. It's a war.[9]

Former residents' accounts of complicity between the 'witdoeke'
and police were substantiated by numerous other eyewitnesses. Jan
van Eck of the PFP Unrest Monitoring Group, for example, publicly
accused certain members of the security forces of actively supporting
the 'witdoeke'.[10] This Captain Jan Calitz vehemently denied:

> Police are continually trying to keep both groups apart by firing
> teargas. We fire teargas into both groups and do everything
> possible to keep the two groups apart. *We categorically deny
> that we are taking sides* [my emphasis].[11]

While 'witdoeke' set up and manned roadblocks along Klipfontein
and Lansdowne Roads, officials from the WCDB began to 'assist'
some of the homeless refugees to move their belongings to an unoccupied piece of land next to Site C in Khayelitsha. They reported
that as many as 79 families had 'voluntarily' moved there in the course
of the day.[12] Most of Portland Cement, Nyanga Bush, and Nyanga
Extension had been burnt to the ground; what little remained was
burnt on the following day by the 'witdoeke'. Many of the refugees,
who were still in the vicinity watching the destruction on Tuesday,
allege that police tried to intimidate them to move to Khayelitsha.

> On Tuesday at about 1.30 p.m. I was standing . . . near the
> [WCDB] offices in Nyanga East. A police van occupied by
> uniformed police drove around the location. The back door of
> the van was open and a white policeman shouted at us that if we
> did not want to go to Khayelitsha they would chase us and kill
> us. The message was in Xhosa, although it was a white man in
> riot police uniform.[13]

Plain-clothes security police also began to harass some of the
refugees who were staying in the nearby Zolani Centre. A woman,
present at the time, felt so intimidated by their actions that she, along
with a number of other refugees, left Zolani to seek safety elsewhere.

> At about 7.30 p.m. [on Tuesday] plain-clothes security forces
> surrounded Zolani Centre. The people outside, most of whom
> were forming queues for soup, stampeded inside. I was knocked
> over onto my back, fortunately I did not harm my youngest
> daughter who was strapped to my back. I then ran into the

centre. There was screaming and crying going on [inside] but a white man wearing blue jeans and a black tracksuit top with 'Indwe' written on the back shouted that if we did not stop screaming and shouting they would kill us there. The people then quietened down. The same man then shouted that they were looking for something, but did not say what. The whole centre was searched including our belongings. Afterwards when we were eating our supper, the centre was surrounded again. Some priests [with us at the time] asked the security forces what they were looking for. They replied that they wanted [someone] called Julia Shangana . . . . [They] then left but returned later. Only they did not come into the centre. [The next day] I left Zolani Centre . . . . [14]

For refugees like Joyce Temba, life in the Cape Peninsula had become, almost overnight, a virtual nightmare. There were now reported to be between 25 and 44 people dead; 3000 shacks burnt; and at least 30 000 refugees from the three satellite camps. Many welfare, church, and community organisations began to rally to their support. By Wednesday, there were at least 17 collection points around the Cape Peninsula from which food, clothing, and blankets donated by a shocked public were distributed. There was also a general outcry from groups like the PFP and the UF for a judicial inquiry into allegations concerning the role of the police and the 'witdoeke'.[15] Most of the general public could not understand what exactly was taking place in the black townships and squatter camps.

A *Cape Times* editorial on 23 May, summed up how some groups were feeling about the situation:

For the [UF] to suggest, even by implication, that the black communities no longer trust the authorities is a chilling indictment. What exactly has been going on in Crossroads? What has led to the violence which has left at least 26 people dead, hundreds injured and some 30 000 [homeless]? The [UF's] statement gives some indication of the complexities. There will be some conflicting opinions, no doubt, on the relative significance of various factors underlying the violence . . . . Neither the [UF] nor anyone else are in a position to comment on the reliability of these allegations [about the role of the police]. Yet the implications are horrifying, suggesting that the guardians of the law are

themselves the sponsors of violence. If this is only partly true, it
suggests that the Botha government is promoting or condoning
legal and moral anarchy, striking at the roots of civilized society.
It is imperative that the facts be established, quickly, by an
impartial tribunal.[16]

The state's response was a public assurance from Chris Heunis to
the effect that his officials were doing everything in their power to
restore peace to the area *and* remove people as quickly as they could to
nearby Khayelitsha. He also made it clear that the area previously
occupied by the satellite camps would soon be prepared for the
upgrading of Old Crossroads. For the WCDB and the Old Crossroads
leadership, their long cherished dream of removing thousands of
'illegal' squatters from the land seemed at last to be fulfilled. Heunis,
during a parliamentary debate, implied that as far as the state was
concerned, unless something was done 'to restore the balance', the
ANC would succeed in making parts of the country ungovernable. He
added that events in Crossroads showed what could happen 'if
diabolical forces' had their own way. Some of the Crossroads people,
he said, were fighting against 'forces of violence and chaos'. There
were forces at work, Heunis continued, trying to prevent 'reform and
co-operation'.[17] Heunis's assertions seemed to confirm the suspicions
of many refugees and the general public: the satellite camps had, in
the final analysis, been destroyed to maintain 'law and order' and enforce control.

To ensure that the upgrading of the devastated area and the removal
of former residents to Khayelitsha continued apace, Heunis appointed
a 'Committee of top officials to deal with the rehabilitation of
Crossroads and the resettlement of refugees'. Timo Bezuidenhoud
was taken off other duties to concentrate on 'the project'.[18] At the
same time that this was announced, WCDB workers were already busy
fencing off the land formerly occupied by the residents of Portland
Cement, Nyanga Bush, and Nyanga Extension with rolls of barbed
wire. There was no doubt in anyone's mind that the state really meant
what it said.

Other Responses

Heunis's announcement on the Crossroads upgrading placed the UF,
who for some time had been negotiating with the Department of

Constitutional Development and Planning to upgrade the entire Crossroads complex for *all* of its inhabitants, into a quandary. There were soon strong rumours that the UF was reassessing its role in the upgrading project, in the light of the announcement and the violence which preceded it. A week later, the UF issued a public statement in which it formally announced its withdrawal from the Crossroads upgrading scheme, detailing reasons for doing so. Given this body's long history of involvement in the area, and the fact that it reflected the thinking of a significant sector of the business community inside the country, it merits close consideration:

> The Foundation has a long history of involvement in Crossroads, both as a mediator and in the development of a number of community-based projects. As a result of this, the Foundation was requested by the committees of the various community groups and by the government to act as a development agency in co-ordinating an upgrade programme . . . . Among the principles identified as being essential for a successful upgrade programme were the right of the residents to remain in Crossroads, the participation of all the inhabitants of Crossroads, and that the planning and implementation process be one of community participation . . . . The Foundation believes that the principles upon which the upgrading will now proceed do not conform with those identified by the Foundation as being essential for the implementation of a successful upgrade programme . . . . [We] therefore regret that [the UF] must at this stage withdraw from further participation in the upgrading of Crossroads.[19]

Crossroads had become a political liability for the UF. Not even monopoly capital could afford to associate itself, and therefore become indirectly implicated, in the events of the last few days. As far as defending the 'witdoeke' and the police were concerned, the state stood on its own.

The UDF and its affiliates were much slower in responding to the crisis in and around the Crossroads complex. Although many activists from progressive organisations assisted the relief agencies as volunteers, the UDF took a full week to issue a public statement, despite the fact that what had happened was a direct and blatant attack on organised resistance to the state. At a mass rally on 25 May in Mitchells Plain, an ANC message of solidarity was read to the

crowd. Christmas Tinto, UDF vice-chairperson, assured those present
that the squatters would not move to Khayelitsha:

> Our people are saying that they will go back [to their land]. They
> will not move to Khayelitsha . . . . The struggle is not
> easy . . . but it will continue . . . .[20]

As time would show, however, this was not a realistic assessment.
The initiative was not in the hands of, nor did it come from, the progressive movement. Already rumours and fears were spreading
through the townships of a possible attack on KTC. This was based
not only on Ndima's earlier threat in April, but also on reports of
searches and warnings to the residents of KTC that their camp would
be burnt unless people moved to Khayelitsha. Gloria Mnqumevu, a
resident of the camp, described one of the raids which took place as
early as 23 May. There was little doubt in the minds of the KTC
residents that, after this attack, their fate would eventually be the
same as that suffered by the former satellite camps. For those who had
taken refuge at KTC following the destruction of their homes, this
possibility must have been almost too much to bear.

> On the morning of Friday 23 May, a large force of policemen
> and army soldiers arrived at KTC squatter camp . . . . Large
> numbers of policemen and soldiers on foot then began moving
> through [the camp] searching many of the shacks in the area.
> [They] told the residents that they were looking for arms and
> other weapons. Most of the residents were [frightened] when the
> policemen and soldiers [came] in such large numbers to our
> camp . . . . [One of the soldiers] approached our group I
> will . . . quote what I remember him saying. 'If you people are
> still here on Monday night we will come . . . and . . . burn your
> houses down. You must all move to Khayelitsha . . . .' I fear
> that soldiers and policemen will come to burn my shack and
> destroy my property . . . .[21]

Over the weekend of 24-25 May, there were a number of incidents
of intimidatory actions on the part of the police — for example, a constant presence of police Casspirs in the area, and teargas being thrown
into KTC between 3 a.m. and 5 a.m. on Sunday. The KTC Committee, called Masincedane, anticipating the possibility of the camp's

destruction as soon as Ndima's threat materialised, had begun to take precautions soon after the destruction of the satellite camps. With the assistance of the Legal Resources Centre (LRC) they began to prepare a court interdict against the state, as well as Ngxobongwana and Ndima, restraining them from unlawfully entering KTC and destroying their camp. Since 20 May, the leaders of KTC, together with Yamile, Toise, Siphika, and scores of residents, eyewitnesses, and others familiar with the Crossroads situation, had spent countless hours preparing and filing affidavits for an interdict. This 'urgent application' was heard in the Supreme Court on 26 May.

There were no responding affidavits contesting the evidence contained in the 45 affidavits filed by the LRC lawyers. Instead a sworn statement from Col. M.G. Mans was presented to the court on behalf of most of the respondents. It argued that the interdict would 'limit and seriously hamper the activities of the security forces . . . and could lead to the necessary withdrawal of all security forces.' This, Mans argued, 'will result in the collapse of law and order and a blood-bath between rival factions'.[22] The presiding judge rejected the state's argument which implied that the conflict in the area was nothing more than 'black on black' violence. A temporary interdict restraining the SAP, SADF, Ngxobongwana and Ndima, from 'unlawful' behaviour was granted on Monday 26 May. The return date given by the court for the state to present its evidence was 13 June.[23] By then, however, KTC would already be destroyed and a State of Emergency declared throughout the country.

The Interim Period

In the period between the court interdict and the attack on KTC, the state continued to press ahead with its plans to upgrade the Crossroads area and resettle the refugees at Khayelitsha. The official estimate of refugees who had moved to the resettlement area was 2500.[24] Thousands were still being given relief in a number of church halls and centres throughout the black townships. Others were rebuilding shacks, or living in tents and makeshift shelters on vacant land in Nyanga East. One such settlement, opposite the home of former UDF president Oscar Mpetha, adopted the name of Mpetha Square. The vast majority of the 30 000-40 000 refugees had, however, somehow disappeared. Many were staying with friends and relatives in the surrounding townships. Numerous appeals and delegations to Heunis, by representatives of the churches and relief agencies, requesting that the state give assistance to the refugees and allow them eventually to return to their land, were flatly rejected. As far as the state was concerned the destruction of the satellite camps had provided it with an opportunity to carry out its policy of 'orderly urbanisation', and it would allow nothing and nobody to turn it from this course. Ken Andrew of the PFP captured the essence of Heunis's hardline attitude:

> You've lost the war. We've got you off the land and we are not letting you back. Unless you go to Khayelitsha, we will do nothing to help you in your awful plight . . . .[25]

The Destruction of KTC

> You can reach out in front of you . . . clench your fist and squeeze fear out of the air . . . .[26]

On the morning of 9 June, in the midst of persistent rumours that the 'witdoeke' and security forces were preparing to attack, the onslaught against refugees in the townships and KTC began. This time, according to many people present at the first attack (10 a.m.), the assistance of the police to the 'witdoeke' was irrefutable.

The attack on KTC and the refugee centres began between 8 and 10 a.m. on Monday, 9 June — four days before the return date of the temporary court interdict. 'Witdoeke' began to gather and prepare for the fight on a piece of land next to the Administration Board offices early that morning. They did so in the presence of police. A KTC resident, Elliot Samuel, guarding the camp at the time, described the initial attacks on the Zolani Centre and KTC in the following way:

> During the evening of Sunday, 8 June, I received a message from the KTC Committee that they had been informed that the Old Crossroads people would attack KTC either that night or the next morning. The committee asked all male residents to stand guard . . . . At about 8 a.m. [on Monday] I heard the sounds of shouting . . . in the area. I . . . went again to stand on the hill behind the church. From [there] I could see clearly . . . a very

large crowd of people standing near the Administration Board offices in Nyanga, near Nontsumba Bush . . . . I saw four or five Casspirs in the immediate vicinity of this crowd. I then rode in a car . . . towards the Administration Board offices . . . I saw clearly then that these men were 'witdoeke' . . . I also saw [about] four or five Casspirs . . . . Standing near [one of the vans] and talking with some of the 'witdoeke' was a policeman I recognised as Barnard. I know this man well . . . . I saw the yellow Casspir start driving along Millers Road (NY5) towards KTC . . . . [T]he large crowd of 'witdoeke' then started following the Casspir. The Casspir was driving very slowly, at walking speed. The 'witdoeke' seemed to be following the Casspir and many of them were armed . . . . The van . . . drove behind the yellow Casspir and the 'witdoeke' in the direction of KTC. [It] appeared to be accompanying the 'witdoeke'. I and my friends then drove ahead of the 'witdoeke' and the [other cars] towards KTC. [We wanted] to warn [the residents] that an attack was [coming] . . . . I was dropped off at the church from where I went to the top of the sand hill. [From here] I could see [what happened next] . . . . Many of the men [from] KTC were standing on the sand hill in order to form [a line of defence]. I saw the yellow Casspir, the 'witdoeke', and the van move in the direction of the Zolani centre.[27]

From the top of the hill near the church, a few hundred yards from KTC, Elliot Samuel saw the 'witdoeke', accompanied by the Casspirs, move towards the Zolani Centre. He and a number of other KTC residents left the hill so as to get a better view of what was about to happen.

I saw the yellow Casspir and the van park close to the Zolani Centre . . . . [T]hen the 'witdoeke' [started] to attack the centre and assault people who were on the grounds . . . . [W]omen and children who had been [staying there] were running out of it. I then saw the centre begin to burn . . . . [A] crowd of [men] advanced on the 'witdoeke' to try to stop them [from] burning down the centre. The 'witdoeke' then began to retreat. I saw shots being fired from the yellow Casspir at the people who were trying to drive off the 'witdoeke'. [This] forced them to retreat. The 'witdoeke' then returned to the centre which continued to

burn . . . . After a while I saw the crowd of 'witdoeke' who had
been attacking the centre . . . move along the road in the direction of NY5 . . . . The 'witdoeke' then stopped at the intersection near KTC. I then saw a man who I thought was Barnard
get out of the van. He appeared to be talking to [them] . . . .
Once the van left the crowd of 'witdoeke' men from KTC began
moving [towards them] . . . . Casspirs in the vicinity [started]
shooting teargas at the KTC residents . . . . [T]eargas was shot
at [those of us] standing on the hill . . . . At about this time I
saw smoke rising from [one] part of KTC . . . . I then saw 'witdoeke' amongst the KTC houses, which were burning . . . .
Many KTC residents, including myself, then began to move our
[possessions] from our [houses] . . . . Later I returned to KTC
and watched the 'witdoeke' . . . burning our houses . . . .[28]

There were numerous reports of police actively participating in the
burning of these houses. Another KTC resident, Goodwin Nyingwa,
claims to have seen police use what he calls 'flame throwers' to set the
houses alight.

Women and children ran out of KTC camp screaming and crying
and leaving their belongings behind. I then saw policemen from
the Casspirs throw objects which I can best describe as flame
throwers onto the shacks which then burst into flames. I also
saw the police shoot several men in the [camp] . . . . I tried to go
forward several times to help but was [constantly stopped] by
police shooting at me. I spent the whole day [at KTC] trying to
help . . . .[29]

Matthew Walton and Lee Bozalek, two lawyers from the LRC who
tried to get into the area on the Monday, were stopped by police at a
roadblock not far from KTC. Their evidence confirms the non-
interventionist role of the police towards the 'witdoeke'. At about 3
p.m. they saw a crowd of 200-300 'witdoeke' pass through the same
police blockade. The group came from the vicinity of the Administration Board offices. According to them, no attempt was made to stop
the 'witdoeke' from moving towards KTC.

[The] police stationed in the vicinity of the intersection did
nothing to stop [the 'witdoeke'] from proceeding towards KTC.

[They] were permitted to proceed along the road past the
vehicles and the roadblock without objection . . . . I was struck
by the fact that the . . . 'witdoeke' appeared undeterred by [the
police presence] . . . . They did not hesitate as they approached
the police and army vehicles but simply walked past them in the
direction of KTC.[30]

The burning and looting continued until 4 p.m. when the 'witdoeke'
left the area, going back in the direction of Old Crossroads. Although
residents from KTC and the nearby townships, especially the youth,
tried to resist the 'witdoek' attack, there was little they could do given
the existing balance of forces. Comrades, who fought running battles
with the 'witdoeke' all day, were instrumental in at least forcing them
to retreat that afternoon. By this time, however, a significant propor-
tion of KTC was already destroyed, as were a number of the nearby
refugee centres. There were also thousands of new refugees. The situation was one of confusion and chaos.

The SAP, forced by the public outcry that followed the news of this
brutal attack on KTC, issued a public statement from the police Direc-
torate in Pretoria, giving the 'official' version of why and how the
events of 9 June occurred.

At approximately 10 a.m. large groups of blacks, allegedly the
so called 'witdoeke' and the comrades, congregated outside the
Administration Board offices at Nyanga. The police warned
them to disperse but they ignored the warning and started
fighting while moving in the direction of KTC. At the KTC
camp a number of structures were set alight and the fire, because
of a strong wind blowing at the time, soon spread to adjoining
structures. The community hall and 3 marquee tents at Zolani
Centre were also destroyed in the blaze. Security forces are at
present in control of the situation.[31]

This time, however, very few found it possible to believe the state's
version of what was really going on inside the black townships. Even
the *Cape Times*, by no means a radical newspaper, began to raise
questions about the possible involvement of a 'dirty tricks squad' in
what they termed a 'sophisticated counter-insurgency operation'.[32]

The attack on KTC continued the next day. This time 'witdoeke'
began gathering at the Nyanga East bus terminus at about 9 a.m. They

were seen with four armed white men in plain clothes.[33] Comrades and
KTC residents began to gather in increasing numbers along a ridge
running through the camp. Police in Casspirs soon were seen firing
teargas and shots at those who had gathered there.[34] Not long after
this, the 'witdoeke' started moving along the road from the burnt out
Zolani Centre towards KTC. They were accompanied by at least seven
Casspirs.[35] Between 12 and 1 p.m. the 'witdoeke' attacked KTC on at
least two occasions. Although residents and comrades inside the area
tried to fight them off, the police, using teargas, made this
impossible.[36] By 1 p.m., KTC was again in flames. Late in the afternoon 'witdoeke' returned to Old Crossroads, leaving behind them
another trail of destruction. They would return again the following
day. In the course of bitter fighting between the 'witdoeke', comrades,
and police on Wednesday, 11 June, George De'ath, a freelance
cameraman for BBC, would become the first newsman to be killed
covering unrest in South Africa.[37] At the end of the twenty-seven day
war, an estimated 100 people were dead and 70 000 were turned into
refugees in the land of their birth.

When P.W. Botha finally declared a general State of Emergency on
12 June, he did so, he said, on the advice of security experts, who
believed 'that the entire Republic [was] a target area . . . for radical
and revolutionary elements'.[38] Thousands of homeless refugees,
caught in the crossfire of raw politics, knew long before this that the
terrain of struggle had already been restructured. In June 1986, they
were once again faced with a struggle to survive and, if possible, resist
a state as determined as they were to maintain control over their lives.
For the remainder of the year, squatter struggles would continue in the
Cape Peninsula, on this new terrain and in the shadow of a State of
Emergency. The last section of this chapter briefly reviews events immediately following the destruction of KTC and more recent strategies
on the part of the state.

June to December 1986 — The Struggle Continues

Although it is difficult to write about the period between the destruction of these squatter camps and the present, given its immediacy and
political fluidity, this book would be incomplete without an attempt to
do so. It tries to capture a sense of the confusion and outrage of those
affected by the events of May — June, amid denials from 'witdoeke'

and the state. It reports on continuing struggles by former residents of Portland Cement, Nyanga Bush and Nyanga Extension not only to survive, but also to reorganise their lives in the face of a vigilant state determined to carry out strategies of reform and repression. Within Old Crossroads itself, the focus is on power struggles between Ngxobongwana supporters and those disaffected by his rule, for one reason or another. The absence of the progressive organisations from this social equation is stark, and cannot be reduced to the State of Emergency alone. In the present, as in the past, squatters face the day to day realities of survival on their own. The political implications of this will be explored in the final chapter.

Chaos, Confusion, and Outrage

In the period immediately following KTC's destruction and the declaration of a State of Emergency on 12 June 1986, there was general outrage and anger locally and abroad. Film footage of the KTC attack, screened on British television on Tuesday 10 June, showed white plain-clothes policemen with 'witdoeke' during the conflict. The BBC highlighted each white man with a tiny spotlight. The SAP acknowledged the presence of plain-clothes policemen in KTC, arguing that they were there 'to speed up investigations into individual killings'.[39] Few were impressed, however, with the consistent denials of some complicity between members of the security forces and 'witdoeke', especially in the light of the previous allegations. A *Cape Times* editorial condemned the KTC attack in no uncertain terms:

> The apparent impotence or, according to reliable eyewitnesses, resolute unwillingness of the authorities to protect hapless refugees and other law-abiding citizens from marauding gangs of vigilantes in KTC, Crossroads and environs is assuming the proportions of a national if not international scandal . . . . The burning questions remain. Have some 50 000 people become homeless as a result of a deliberate decision to exploit communal tensions and promote factional hostilities? By whom would such a decision have been taken and executed? To what purpose? For the sake of counter-insurgency operations against the so-called 'comrades'? Or a forced mass removal to Khayelitsha? Is this a new and particularly ghastly technique of removal? . . .

[N]either police nor military have been effectively deployed to
keep the peace. Why has this been so? Has someone made a
ghastly error of judgement? Was this deliberate, carefully considered policy, supported at a high level? The public is entitled to
know . . . .[40]

While the outcry continued, the situation within the areas surrounding the KTC and Crossroads war zone remained tense. Rumours were
rife that the 'witdoeke' were preparing to attack New Crossroads, as
well as other townships. Anyone suspected of living in Old Crossroads
or Site C — seen as 'witdoek' territory — entered the nearby
townships at their own risk.[41] Isolated incidents of conflict between
'witdoeke', militant comrades, and angry residents jeopardised
Bishop Tutu's efforts to negotiate a truce between the warring groups.
Tutu, after separate meetings with Sam Ndima and the 'witdoeke' at
Site C, as well as with the squatter leaders and representatives of progressive organisations, managed at least to get both sides to agree to a
ceasefire. 'Peace talks' were also scheduled to take place on 21 June.[42]
But with feelings running high for revenge on all sides, these initiatives
remained limited.

Four days after KTC's destruction, the real meaning of South
African justice was highlighted when the KTC interdict, initially
granted to restrain the SAP, SADF and 'witdoeke' from unlawfully
entering the area, was extended.[43] A hearing was set for 8 August at
which both sides would present oral evidence to the court. Although
this offered an opportunity to the former squatter residents publicly to
expose much of the evidence and allegations against police and 'witdoeke', it was of little comfort to the thousands of KTC refugees who
poured into mosques, churches, and community centres all over the
Cape Peninsula in the aftermath of the attack. Yet even there, they
would find little refuge. Even while bulldozers were clearing wreckage
from the devastated KTC camp, 5000 refugees, staying in six schools
in Nyanga and Guguletu, were given a week to vacate the premises.
Mosques and churches in other areas were likewise served notices in
terms of the Black Urban Areas Act of 1945, and told that they would
be charged with a criminal offence unless the refugees left these
centres.[44] This Act, used to hound the refugees, had in fact been re-
pealed in parliament as part of the state's latest reform programme. A
refugee from KTC captured the sham of Botha's much publicised
scrapping of the pass laws:

> President Botha's reforms mean nothing when we have nowhere
> to stay. I've got a pass but no home. What's the good of that? [45]

The spirit of survival and resistance of many former squatter
residents was not yet crushed, despite the brutal destruction of their
communities. Reports soon filtered out of the area of 'frantic
building' in KTC, as hundreds of determined KTC residents started
moving back to reoccupy the devastated area. Within ten days, an
estimated 1000 homes had been rebuilt.[46] The state too showed its
determination. On 22 June, Brigadier Swart, Divisional Commissioner of Police in the Western Cape. issued an order in terms of the
Public Safety Act prohibiting members of the public, including the
press, from entering KTC, the Crossroads complex, Nyanga and New
Crossroads. In a further order, this time issued in terms of the
emergency regulations, Swart forbade people who had fled KTC from
returning there, or rebuilding their homes.[47] Hundreds of squatters
ignored this, refusing to be intimidated into 'voluntarily' moving into
Khayelitsha. By mid-July there were over 6000 squatters back on the
KTC site, living in damaged houses.[48] Thousands more dreamed of
one day returning to their land. This, they knew, would necessitate
struggle not only against the state, but also against the residents and
leaders of Old Crossroads, both of whom, for different reasons,
wanted the land cleared of squatters. Ngxobongwana, back in Old
Crossroads after a three-month 'leave of absence', told the squatters
in no uncertain terms that the reoccupation of the land was a non-
negotiable issue:

> [These squatters] can never come back. It belongs to the people
> of Crossroads. Mr Bezuidenhoud *is* prepared to give them a safe
> place, but they are not prepared to go . . . . Yamile, Toise and
> Siphika must take what the government offers . . . .[49]

Who would control the land of the Crossroads complex remained a
contested issue amongst the former residents of the satellite camps,
the leadership of Old Crossroads, and the South African state.

Denials

There were reports that many Old Crossroads residents were unhappy
with what had taken place between their community and the squatter

camps. Although it is not possible to verify this development, given limited access to information, there is no doubt that there was considerable pressure on the Old Crossroads leadership from residents of their own community and outside groups to justify their actions against the surrounding squatter settlements. In July the Executive Committee issued a statement, not to my knowledge covered by the press, which detailed events leading up to the fight. It also challenged the media for having presented only one side of the story. It is one of the few accounts given by the 'witdoeke' of their reasons for the conflict.

> We in Crossroads under Mr Ngxobongwana are now making a public statement about the fighting in our territory. The fight started heavily on Saturday evening 17 May after Mr Ntshangana a squatter leader associated with Mr Ngxobongwana was attacked by Mr Siphika. This he [did] for the second time [after being warned about it] at a meeting in Site C. We attacked Mr Toise [for supporting Siphika] and some of his men ran to Mr Yamile, another squatter leader. Early Sunday morning youth from [Yamile's camp] came with some men and fired shots and threw petrol bombs at Mr Gunuzan's shop and houses in [Section 4]. Thirty houses were immediately burnt down . . . . Later our men in fury fought back attacking and burning shacks in Yamile's [area]. We allowed women and children from these shacks to come out as we did not [consider them to be guilty]. We and our people . . . have been attacking and consequently destroying forces from these neighbouring squatter leaders which [have been] attacking and killing our people indiscriminately.[50]

The statement then details some of the main reasons why the Executive believed fighting erupted in the Crossroads complex:

> The fight mostly stems from the issue of the upgrading of Crossroads . . . . Mr Ngxobongwana had written a letter to Mr Chris Heunis asking for the starting of [the upgrading scheme] as the circumstances in the area are worrying . . . . [T]his letter in a way not known to us [was shown] to Mr Siphika, Yamile, and Toise who then became angry [about] it. We then called them to meetings several times . . . to clear up the misunderstandings but they refused to come. We asked Mr Hoza at

Site C to invite leaders to a meeting in his area. Others would come, but Mr Yamile would not. After an argument about the letter to Mr Chris Heunis, Mr Siphika who claimed we were opposed to [them being] in Crossroads openly [threatened] to attack Crossroads . . . . Mr Yamile had also before threatened to crush Crossroads. He had boasted [of being] the sole leader of Crossroads because he had heavy weapons from Russia.

Trouble between us and our neighbouring squatter leaders has been encouraged further by some previous Executive members who held meetings with these leaders against Crossroads. One of them Mr Naphakade cut ground for Mr Yamile which was under our headman Mr Mazele. Our people cried to us against Mr Yamile. We were challenged to fight. Our leader's life, Mr Ngxobongwana, is highly sought after by these leaders and their youth. His house has been bombed several times but without harm . . . . [He] has been accused of being against organizations. This followed what he said in court [during] his trial where he said Crossroads was not obtained by means of organizations. This he said to settle a query from the people about his lawyer when some favoured the lawyers [of] the UDF . . . . When he denounced the burning of people he became unacceptable to some organizations, especially the youth. [Sometimes] up to three people would be found burnt in the mornings in Crossroads. Our case has been interfered [with] by some organizations which want to control forcefully. This has brought the involvement of the police who say they are here to check on disturbances caused by comrades. We are now looking after our place because we struggled for it . . . . We are keeping watch [at] all times because there are evils done on us which are not said. We have much stated our account since we do not have the opportunity to do so in official newspapers . . . . [They] have shown preference [rather] than open service to the whole society. This goes for other agencies who are influenced against us by certain elements from our communities. Even aid has been withheld by these agencies to our people through this influence. But we are here for those who wish to know.[51]

Tensions and pressures inside Old Crossroads have taken their toll. Divisions have emerged within its leadership. In Ngxobongwana's absence (March — June) the political vacuum was of necessity filled

other leaders. Prince Gobingca, who moved to Old Crossroads after the December/January 1986 conflict in New Crossroads,
appears to have established a power base from which to challenge
Ngxobongwana's leadership. Many former residents of Old Crossroads, familiar with the politics of their former community, predict
violence inside the area.[52] In a community where power has for the last
seven years been centralised in one man's hands — Ngxobongwana's
— and where all challenges to this have been met with brute force, one
can expect that the taking of power now, as in the past, will result in
more violence and conflict.

The KTC Court Hearing

The Old Crossroads version of the reasons for the May — June conflict was, to a large extent, supported by the responding affidavits filed
by police, security police, and various state officials in preparation for
the August hearing of the KTC interdict. Louis Le Grange, however,
denied all parties the chance to tell the various sides of the story. In a
surprise development, he refused to oppose the granting of a final
order restraining the state and 'witdoeke' from attacking KTC. This
meant that no evidence would be presented in court. Le Grange
argued in an affidavit presented minutes before the case was to begin
(8 August), that the matter had now become 'academic' since most of
KTC had already been destroyed. Other reasons he cited for not want-
ing to go to court were that the case would run for months, costing
taxpayers thousands of rands, and that members of the security forces
would be kept away from their 'duties'.[53]

In a joint statement issued by the squatter leaders a few days later,
they announced their intention to sue the state for damages, claiming
that Le Grange's actions were tantamount to an admission of guilt:

> The reason [Le Grange] did not stand up in court against us is
> because he did not want the whole world to know what happened
> . . . . [T]he government must pay for the damage they caused.
> Our brothers and sisters have died; our property, our houses,
> our furniture, shops and businesses are destroyed. We must be
> paid.[54]

In a situation where all sides felt aggrieved and misunderstood, one could anticipate a residue of bitterness and anger. Although thousands of the former residents of the satellite camps and KTC have since officially sued the Minister of Law and Order for R5 000 000 damages, no amount of money can compensate for the destruction of these communities. This remains an account still to be settled.[55]

Ongoing Survival and Resistance

For those who found themselves homeless refugees as a result of the political and military power struggles of May — June, life remains a tough and bitter struggle for survival. Thousands have resisted attempts to make them move 'voluntarily' to Khayelitsha. Many began to trickle back to the townships during July and August, no longer able, or willing, to live as refugees in churches and mosques. They moved onto whatever piece of unoccupied land they could find. New squatter settlements have mushroomed all over Nyanga. Mpetha and Butter Square, to name two, soon became home to a hard core of former residents of the Crossroads complex and KTC. As has happened so often in the past, homeless squatters occupied and cleared new land for survival.

Thousands of others, tired of the continual pressure to move to Khayelitsha and the ever present fear of further conflict erupting, slowly moved to a rapidly growing tent town next to Site C, nicknamed 'Green Point'.[56] By the middle of September an estimated 126 000 people were living at Khayelitsha.[57] Many moved there in the hope that they and their families would somehow find peace.

But, for the thousands who continue their struggle from these new squatter settlements, as well as those who presently inhabit the surrounding townships and Khayelitsha, the future looks far from promising. New citizenship laws recently passed as part of the state's 'reform' programme could, according to members of the Black Sash, mean that as many as 700 000 black people in the Western Cape are, in terms of the new laws, 'aliens' and therefore not entitled to either housing or jobs in the region.[58] The signs that life will become worse and not better for those without proper housing or jobs are already visible.

At the end of October, officials from the new Community Services Office of the Cape Administration began taking a census of illegal structures in Nyanga, Langa, and Guguletu for what was termed 'future planning purposes'. The pattern of formulating strategies of control over the city's black population is being repeated. Refugee shelters in the new squatter settlements, as well as backyard shacks, were included in the census.[59] The long-term objectives of this were made crystal clear by officials from Community Services:

> We need the information for future planning in the light of the Government's new orderly urbanisation policy.[60]

In April 1986, when the state announced the abolition of influx control, Heunis emphasised that this did not mean that the country was 'heading for a period of chaotic growth of cities and town'.[61] The May — June events in the squatter camps of the Cape Peninsula, as well as subsequent events, demonstrate that reform is merely the flipside of the coin in South African politics. Repression has consistently kept pace with the state's reformist initiatives. In the present South African context it is clear that reform cannot proceed without repression.

Maintaining 'Law and Order'

To ensure that 'law and order' was maintained in the townships, power was devolved to a new SAP task force called 'special constables', nicknamed 'kitskonstabels' (instant police) by local township residents. This new unit has been deployed in some areas 'to make the long arm of the law a little bit longer'.[62] New recruits consist of hundreds of former 'witdoeke', as well as former 'comrades'. Now, however, they are *legally* armed with sjamboks and guns, and let loose to deal with 'trouble-makers' in the black townships.

The first weekend that the 'kitskonstabels' arrived back in the townships from their six-week training course, they were already under attack from residents and comrades. In New Crossroads there were reports of at least 18 guns being taken from them in the course of their first week 'on the beat'.[63] These 'kitskonstabels' have now been placed alongside community councillors as sell outs and symbols of black oppression. The tragedy is that most of them, like the 'witdoeke', are merely pawns in a game whose ground rules are ultimately controlled by the South African state. In the conflict-ridden Cape Peninsula, where 'orderly urbanisation' strategies — fundamentally issues of state security — continue in the shadow of an ongoing State of Emergency, resistance and repression remain predictable.

Notes

1. *Cape Times*, 19.5.1986.
2. Selina Valo, Affidavit.
3. Kululekile Mdlalana, Affidavit.
4. Violet Voyiya, Affidavit.
5. Simour Menziwa, Affidavit.
6. Alfred Siphika, Affidavit.
7. *Cape Times*, 20.5.1986.
8. Ibid.
9. *Argus*, 20.5.1986.
10. *Cape Times*, 20.5.1986.
11. Ibid.
12. Ibid.
13. Joyce Temba, Affidavit.
14. Ibid.
15. *Cape Times*, 22.5.1986.
16. Ibid.
17. Ibid. 22.5.1986.
18. *Argus*, 23.5.1986.
19. *Cape Times*, 30.5.1986.
20. Ibid., 26.5.1986.
21. Gloria Mnqumevu, Affidavit.
22. *Cape Times*, 27.5.1986.
23. Ibid.
24. Ibid., 31.5.1986.
25. Ibid., 6.6.1986.
26. *Argus*, 10.6.1986.
27. Elliot Samuel, Affidavit.
28. Ibid.
29. Goodwin Nyingwa, Affidavit.
30. Matthew Walton, Affidavit.
31. *Cape Times*, 10.6.1986.
32. Ibid.
33. D. Bosman, Affidavit.
34. Ibid.
35. Ibid.
36. Rev. J. Freeth, Affidavit.
37. George De'ath died from head wounds sustained from being hit over the head with axes and pangas.
38. *Cape Times*, 13.6.1986.
39. *Argus*, 12.6.1986.
40. *Cape Times*, 11.6.1986.
41. This information is based on informal discussions with a minister from the townships who monitored the situation carefully during this period. Although none of the ongoing incidents of conflict were reported by the press, due to a news blackout following the State of Emergency, there were reports of a number of

suspected 'witdoeke' being necklaced and/or abducted by comrades in the course of the rest of June.

42. *Cape Times*, 13.6.1986.
43. Ibid.
44. Ibid., 20.6.1986.
45. Ibid., 24.6.1986.
46. Ibid., 21.6.1986.
47. Ibid., 23.6.1986.
48. Ibid., 18.7.1986.
49. Ibid., 24.7.1986.
50. 'Now Crossroads Account About The Fighting', issued by the Crossroads Executive Committee (July, 1986).
51. Ibid.
52. Based on informal discussions with former Old Crossroads Executive members who have been monitoring the situation carefully over the past few months (June — November).
53. Ibid., 8.8.1986.
54. Ibid., 12.6.1986.
55. Over 3 300 squatters, with the assistance of the LRC and Department of Criminology, UCT, filed damages in separate court cases, totalling over R5 000 000. The squatters alleged in their summonses against the SAP, that members of the police force 'made common cause with and assisted inter alia the said persons [witdoeke] from Old Crossroads in destroying and/or causing the loss of the said dwelling and property'. See *Cape Times*, 12.11.1986, for a fuller report.
56. Green Point is a suburb of Cape Town.
57. *Cape Times*, 18.9.1986.
58. Ibid., 23.9.1986.
59. The WCDB came to an official end in June, becoming Community Services. Its various functions were to be parcelled out to different government departments at the end of the year.
60. *Cape Times*, 29.10.1986.
61. Chris Heunis, Press Release, following the tabling of the White Paper on Urbanisation, 23.4.1986.
62. *Cape Times*, 22.9.1986.
63. New Crossroads, Interview No. 4 (1986).

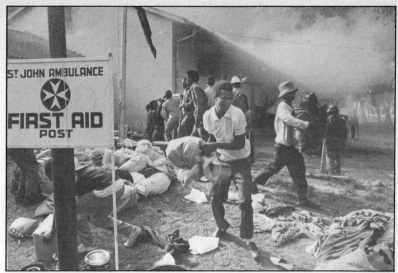

Afrapix

Afrapix

32   *The Zolani Centre refugees under attack (June 1986).*

33   *KTC Burns (June 1986).*

Afrapix

Afrapix

34 *Refugees begin to rebuild shelters — Browns Farm, opposite the
Crossroads Complex (August 1986).*

35 *'Green Point', Khayelitsha, becomes the new 'home' for hundreds of
squatter refugees (1986).*

36 *Johnson Ngxobongwana, government-backed leader of Old Crossroads, and his supporters (1986).*

37   The coming of the special constables, nicknamed the 'kitskonstabels' (November 1986).

Chapter 11

Overview and Conclusions

This book has tried to capture something of the tragedy, complexity, and contradictions which define squatter history in the Western Cape. It is a story which constantly alludes to both the formation and the destruction of squatter communities. Focussing on the eleven-year history of one particular community, as well on as other squatter settlements which emerged during the 1980s, highlights the complex interplay between changing state strategies and struggles taking place on the ground. A particular concern of this book has been to try to understand why and how Crossroads, once a symbol of resistance and defiance, eventually aligned itself with the South African state to destroy nearby squatter communities in 1986. The answers to these questions are woven into the community's own contradictory history, as well as into the wider political context within which Crossroads residents found themselves situated. In the final analysis, the history of Crossroads is a story about the politics of everyday life in South Africa. It corresponds closely to the experiences of thousands of other people who survive and resist oppression as squatters in South Africa. Yet this history is also unique. Few communities in this country have been subjected to as much pressure, or have influenced the trajectory of politics — on the ground and at the level of the state — as has Crossroads.

The Early Years

In the context of state attempts to restructure African settlement in the Cape Peninsula during the mid-1970s, Crossroads emerged as one of a number of squatter camps. Its formation was the outcome of a dual process — on the one hand, continuing state initiatives to control the surplus African population and, on the other, the determination of a small group of residents who, through one social route or another, found themselves struggling to survive on a piece of land near Nyanga East. In the 1970s, these first residents fought a tenacious battle to remain on the land. After two years of raids and legal struggles, Crossroads eventually won the right to remain as an Emergency Camp. From 1976 until 1978, when the community faced the next major threat to its existence, Crossroads established and consolidated much of its social infrastructure. The structures the residents created were distinctive and drew on prior experiences and beliefs. Power structures reflected the urban and rural experiences of its inhabitants. In Crossroads these two traditions merged. Although internal power struggles were not absent from the community, they were limited and therefore easily contained. This, as we have seen, changed with time and circumstance.

The Politics of Reform

The second phase of squatter history described in this book began with the onslaught against potential political flashpoints in the wake of the 1976 uprisings. In early 1978, following the destruction of Unibel, Modderdam, and Werkgenot, Crossroads was the only surviving African squatter camp of a major size in Cape Town. The determination of its residents, and the actions of the Crossroads support group throughout most of 1978, resulted in the community winning a 'reprieve' from a state caught in its own contradictions. But the Crossroads 'reprieve' had its cost. Piet Koornhof's intervention set off a chain of new dynamics, as well as reviving old ones. After the negotiations and settlement of 1979, Crossroads found itself caught up in the politics of reform. For a long time to come, the state and representatives of capital were the most significant influencing factors on both the consciousness and the political practice of the community's leadership.

The new political alliance which emerged in 1979, led by Johnson Ngxobongwana, reflected some of these new dynamics. Ngxobongwana would dominate the history of this community for the next seven years. After the Koornhof intervention, power struggles became endemic in Crossroads. In the period immediately following the 'reprieve', the women found themselves defeated by the men of their community. This was a pivotal point in Crossroads history. Their defeat signalled a victory for the state, as well as for patriarchal, petty-bourgeois values. Never again would the women of Crossroads, or the residents as a whole, have the space within which to determine day to day decisions affecting their lives. From 1979 onwards power was concentrated in the hands of a few.

In the context of a physically and politically restructured community, Crossroads residents were ruled by a local black authority which concerned itself more and more with its own material benefits and less and less with the problems of the ordinary residents. As a result, social stratification in Crossroads became stark. While Ngxobongwana and his local community officials accumulated capital, the ordinary residents suffered. Anyone who challenged this, as happened in 1979 and again in 1983, was met with brute force. Community conflicts during the period 1979-1983, represented in the press as 'faction fights', were in essence struggles over who would control the political economy of Crossroads. By the end of 1983, Ngxobongwana and his supporters had complete hegemony over both Old and New Crossroads.

Changing Political Dynamics

The growth of new squatter settlements in the 1980s, again the outcome of state initiatives to maintain control over the Cape Peninsula's African population, together with the rise of community organisation and mobilisation, affected the political trajectory of Old and New Crossroads. In the early 1980s, consistent pressure on the state from local squatter communities, and a growing progressive movement of anti-apartheid forces, became a catalyst to reformist and repressive strategies. This was particularly true as regards policies of influx control.

When Koornhof, after months of unsuccessful attempts by local state officials to contain squatter resistance in the Cape Peninsula, announced the building of Khayelitsha in 1983, he not only sparked off a new wave of resistance but also forced the Crossroads leadership to align itself more openly with nearby squatter settlements and progressive organisations. With the formation of the UDF (1983), the objective conditions were present for the politicisation of squatter resistance in the Cape Peninsula. This, as we have seen, was not without its own specific contradictions. The UDF, in its attempts to mobilise and challenge the state, opted for a strategic alliance with the leadership of the largest squatter community under threat of removal — Crossroads. At the time, this alliance suited both parties — for the Ngxobongwana leadership it entrenched political legitimacy; for the UDF and its affiliates, it strengthened their position vis-a-vis the South African state. For some of the residents of Old and New Crossroads who had become victims of oppression at the hands of a leadership now being publicly embraced by UDF and its affiliates, it only intensified their political confusion. The full implications of this pragmatic alliance would surface in the course of 1985/1986.

During 1984, the state was forced to acknowledge the de facto presence of thousands of 'illegal' squatters living in and around Old and New Crossroads. Following the 'July moratorium' for the Nyanga Bush squatters, thousands of people moved into KTC and the Crossroads complex. Who would control the land and those who inhabited it, remained a burning issue. In the ensuing months a variety of leaders from Nyanga Bush, Nyanga Extension, the Cathedral Group, the newly established Portland Cement camp, as well as Ngxobongwana, vied for control over land and resources. All of them faced the pressure of a state increasingly alarmed at the level of resistance and intent on regaining control over these areas. During 1985, a year which signalled a major political and economic crisis for the country as a whole, squatter struggles became highly politicised. The state, on the defensive, intensified its search for ways to restructure the political terrain.

The Crisis of 1985

In the first half of 1985, resistance in the squatter camps, as well as in other black communities, escalated in the Cape Peninsula. New Crossroads, the focus of conflict between militant activists from UDF-affiliated organisations and community councillors in January, became the first black community to reflect the level of frustration and anger present within Cape Town's black communities. The rent struggle in New Crossroads marked the height of the Ngxobongwana/ UDF alliance. In the course of it, Ngxobongwana would be jailed along with activists from UDF-affiliated organisations. His arrest signalled the beginning of the end of the alliance.

While Ngxobongwana remained in jail, other dynamics were in

play. A rumour in February of a 'removal squad' in Khayelitsha sparked off a wave of unrest within the Crossroads complex. The vanguard role played by militant youth in this conflict created a crisis of control for both the leadership of Old Crossroads and the state. While UDF activists searched for ways to consolidate their new gains in both Old and New Crossroads, the state looked for ways to divide and rule. After Timo Bezuidenhoud successfully split the solidarity of squatter resistance to the removal to Khayelitsha by offering the various communities 18-month permits provided they moved to Site C, the state concentrated on ways to continue its divide and rule strategies. In 1985, it found a willing ally in Johnson Ngxobongwana.

As soon as CAYCO youth and UWO women began to question the political practice of the leadership in Old and New Crossroads, they implicitly challenged Ngxobongwana's rule in these areas. When he returned to Old Crossroads following his acquittal in June, Ngxobongwana immediately went on the offensive in order to regain control over the community. From this moment onwards the battle lines were drawn between him and the progressive organisations. Throughout the remainder of the year, the Ngxobongwana leadership consistently challenged militant activists trying to gain political control over Old and New Crossroads. The consumer boycott and Black Christmas — UDF campaigns, neither of which were well disciplined — gave the Ngxobongwana leadership an opportunity to mobilise reactionaries and ordinary residents against the progressive organisations. This they needed if they were to regain control over Old and New Crossroads.

Continuing unrest between June and October forced the state to extend its State of Emergency to the Western Cape on 26 October. The objectives of the state — to smash organised resistance, and therefore the UDF and its affiliates, as well as to remove thousands of 'illegal' squatters from the Crossroads complex — increasingly coincided with the objectives of a threatened Crossroads leadership. When Chris Heunis announced that R2 million had been set aside for the upgrading of the area, the Ngxobongwana leadership acquired an additional material imperative to re-establish its legitimacy in the area. After December 1985, both of these groupings embarked on a major offensive against militant activists living in the Crossroads complex, resulting in a heightened level of conflict. The seeds of the destruction of the satellite communities and KTC were sown at this date.

The Politics of Repression

As I have tried to show, the destruction of these communities in the period May — June 1986 had been in the making for some time. When nine of Ngxobongwana's men were killed in New Crossroads in March, and two policemen killed in the Crossroads complex shortly afterwards, the balance of forces tilted against activists from progressive organisations. From this point onwards, the Ngxobongwana leadership, led by the head of the Old Crossroads community police Sam Ndima, appears to have actively thrown in its lot with local security forces.

Between April and 17 May 1986, Old and New Crossroads became the focal point of power struggles on a scale never before experienced in these areas. During this period, political activists and residents critical of the Ngxobongwana regime were forced to flee Old Crossroads. At the same time a number of known supporters of Ngxobongwana living in New Crossroads were driven out of the area. Militant activists from both of these communities were, however, incorrect in their assessment of their own strength. By mid-1986 the balance of power was not in their favour. As a result they failed both politically and militarily to out-manouevre the forces pitted against them. The destruction of the satellite camps and KTC in May — June clearly demonstrated this. In a series of bold strokes, the most militant squatter communities and their support group of political activists from UDF and its affiliates suffered a major political and military defeat. The largely unorganised residents of the satellite camps and KTC, caught in the crossfire, proved to be no match for the 'witdoek'/ state alliance. An already weakened progressive movement, faced with another State of Emergency, could offer little support.

Conclusions

By the end of 1986, the political terrain of the Cape Peninsula had been radically restructured by a state determined to maintain control over the majority of its black population. The Crossroads complex, a focal point of squatter resistance to the state, no longer exists. As a result of a political tragedy thousands of its former residents were dispersed throughout the black townships in small squatter settlements. Others, having no other alternative, moved to a variety of site and service camps in Khayelitsha. Old Crossroads, formerly a crucible of resistance, became the apple in the eye of the South African state and a monument to its co-optive strategies.

Community formation and destruction have, as we have seen, long traditions in the Western Cape. Squatter struggles of the 1970s and 1980s in this region visibly demonstrate this process — the outcome of structural conditions, as well as social agency. This history, with its blatant examples of divide and rule strategies from without, and from within these communities, poses a challenge to those people committed to the social transformation of South Africa. It contains invaluable lessons for those who continue to dream of, and actively work towards, social justice and democracy. Crossroads' history illuminates the consistent failure of progressive forces to fundamentally win the hearts and minds of those who lead and inhabit squatter communities on a large scale. That a significant number of workers from these squatter communities and nearby townships actively aligned themselves with the state against respresentatives of the progressive movement is a fact which cannot be wished away. Neither can the rise of right-wing vigilante movements here, as well as in the country as a whole. These are issues which necessitate explanations. The history described in this book shows that reducing them to state strategies alone merely mystifies the reality on the ground and results in political defeats for those who seek social transformation. A crucial political question facing political activists in the Western Cape, is how one mobilises and organises in the light of this contradictory reality.

Here, where a rapidly rising African population is neither organised nor politicised, progressive organisations and trade unions face major obstacles. Unless progressive forces consistently analyse the past and present political terrain and base their actions on this, they will find it difficult to win the hearts and minds of the unorganised masses and thus they will allow the forces of reaction to gain the upper hand. This is the fundamental lesson of the destruction of Crossroads and the satellite camps. An economic recession which increasingly forces many black workers to take up jobs in state structures merely compounds an already difficult situation. The 'kitskonstabels' are a present manifestation of this process. An ongoing State of Emergency also minimises contact between progressive organisations, political activists and the rank and file. The way in which the forces of opposition respond to these challenges will ultimately determine who will win the battle for political legitimacy and control. In the final analysis, this is what the struggle for Crossroads was, and still is, all about.

The history I have tried to capture raises more questions than answers. But the answers, I believe, are hidden within this history. They are there for those who seek to find them. For the countless thousands of ordinary people who experienced the bitter pain of the eleven years covered in this book, and who continue their struggles of survival and resistance, this story is more than just words on paper. For such readers, it is written in the blood of the many who gave their lives for a freedom not yet won.

Bibliography

This bibliography has been divided into:

I UNPUBLISHED SOURCES

A Official
1) *Reports*
2) *Letters*
3) *Memoranda*
4) *Press Statements*

B Non-official
1) *Transcripts of Meetings*

II PUBLISHED SOURCES

A Newspapers and Periodicals

B Pamphlets

C Other

III INTERVIEWS

IV SELECT SECONDARY SOURCES

A Books

B Published Articles and Theses

C Unpublished Articles and Theses

1 UNPUBLISHED SOURCES

A Official

1) *Reports*
Athlone Advice Office Reports, 1979-1982.
Black Sash Report on the Survey.

2) *Letters*
Timo Bezuidenhoud to Crossroads Executive Committee, 12.12.1979.
Crossroads Executive Committee to Department of Community Development, 13.12.1979.
I.M. Russell, Movsowitz and Kahn, to Mr Basson, Superintendent of Bantu Administration Board, 27.1.1982.

3) *Memoranda*
'Memorandum on Crossroads', September, 1981.

4) *Press Statements*
Timo Bezuidenhoud, Chief Commissioner of the Western Cape, 30.9.1982.
Crossroads Executive Committee, 'Now Crossroads' Account About the Fighting', July, 1986.

B Non-Official

1) *Transcripts of Meetings:*
  (i) Urban Foundation and Representatives of Sizamile and Noxolo Committees, 28.9.1978.
  (ii) Urban Foundation and Representatives of Sizamile and Noxolo Committees, 6.11.1978.
  (iii) Minutes of Meeting between Dr. Koornhof and Crossroads Delegation, January, 1979.
  (iv) Minutes of Meeting between Dr. Koornhof and Crossroads Delegation, February, 1979.
  (v) Minutes of Meeting between Dr. Koornhof and Crossroads Delegation, March, 1979.
  (vi) Minutes of Meeting between Crossroads Joint Committee and Urban Foundation, 1.4.1979.
  (vii) Minutes of Meeting between Crossroads Joint Committee and Dr. Koornhof, 1.4.1979.
  (viii) Minutes of Meeting of Crossroads Youth, 7.5.1979.
  (ix) Minutes of Crossroads Joint Committee, 7.5.1979.
  (x) Minutes of Crossroads Joint Committee, 11.7.1979.
  (xi) Minutes of Old Crossroads Executive Committee, 14.2.1980.
  (xii) Minutes of Old Crossroads Executive Committee, 23.3.1982.

II PUBLISHED SOURCES

A Newspapers and Periodicals

The Argus
Cape Times
Die Burger
Financial Mail

B Pamphlets

The Struggle in New Crossroads (UWO, Cape Town, 1985).

C Other

Hansard

III INTERVIEWS

(i) Old Crossroads, 1979.
(ii) Old Crossroads, 1981.
(iii) Regina Ntongana, 1983.
(iv) Old Crossroads, No. 1-7, 1984.
(v) Nyanga Bush, 1984.
(vi) Noel Robb, 1984.
(vii) Khayelitsha, 1985.
(viii) New Crossroads, 1985.
(xi) Old Crossroads, No. 1-4, 1986.
(x) New Crossroads, No. 1-4, 1986.
(xi) Christopher Toise, 1986.

IV SELECT SECONDARY SOURCES

A Books

Bozzoli, B. (Ed.), *Town and Countryside in the Transvaal* (Johannesburg, 1983).
Clarke, J., Critcher C. and Johnson R., Centre for Contemporary Working Class Culture, *Studies in Cultural Studies, History and Theory* (London, 1979).
Hall S. and Jefferson T., *Resistance through Rituals* (Birmingham, 1977).
Haysom N., *Mabangalala* (Johannesburg, 1985).
Kiewet K. and Weichel K., *Inside Crossroads* (Cape Town, 1981).
Marks S. and Rathbone A. (Eds.), *Industrialisation and Social Change in*

South Africa (London, 1982).

NUSAS, *Would You Make a Deal with this Man?* (Cape Town, 1979).

— *The Nyanga Bush Struggle* (Cape Town, 1975).

Russell D., *Crossroads Squatter Camp* (Cape Town, 1975).

Silk A., *A Shanty Town in South Africa: The Story of Modderdam* (Johannesburg, 1981).

Simkins C., *Four Essays on the Past, Present and Possible Futures of the Black Population of South Africa* (Cape Town, 1983).

Surplus People Project, Western Cape, *Khayelitsha: New Home — Old Story* (Cape Town, 1984).

B Published Articles and Theses

Bundy C., 'South Africa on Switchback', *New Society* (London, 1986).

Cole J., 'When Your Life Is Bitter You Do Something', South African Research Paper, Kaplan, D (Ed.) (Cape Town, 1986).

Cornell J. and Maree J., 'Sample Survey of Squatters in Crossroads, December 1977', SALDRU Working Paper, no. 17 (Cape Town, 1978).

Dewar D. and Watson V., 'Urbanisation, Unemployment and Petty Commodity Production and Trading: Comparative Cases in Cape Town', *Living under Apartheid*, Smith D.M.(Ed.) (London, 1981).

Ellis G., 'Africans in the Western Cape: A Chronology', SALDRU Working Paper, no. 50 (Cape Town, 1983).

Eiselen W.,'The Coloured People and the Native', *Journal of Racial Affairs*, 1955.

Gelb S. and Saul J., 'The Crisis in South Africa: Class Defense, Class Revolution', *Monthly Review*, XXXIII, no. 3, 1981.

Goldin I., 'The Poverty of Coloured Labour Preference: Economics and Ideology in the Western Cape', SALDRU Working Paper, no. 59 (Cape Town, 1984).

Hobsbawm E., 'Introduction: Inventing Traditions', *The Invention of Tradition*, Hobsbawm, E. and Ranger, T. (Eds.), (Cambridge, 1984).

Koch E., 'Without Visible Means of Subsistence: Slumyard Culture in Johannesburg 1918-1940', Bozzoli, B (Ed.), *Town and Countryside in the Transvaal* (Johannesburg, 1983).

O'Meara D., 'Muldergate and the Politics of Afrikaner Nationalism', *Work in Progress*, no. 22, 1982.

Saunders C., 'Not Newcomers', *South African Outlook*, 1978.

C Unpublished Articles and Theses

Budow M., 'Urban Squatting in Greater Cape Town, 1939-1948', BA Hons thesis, University of Cape Town, 1976.

Cole J., 'From Community to Mini-Bantustan', BA Hons thesis, University of Cape Town, 1986.

Kinkead-Weekes B., 'Africans in Cape Town: The Origins and Development of State Policy and Popular Resistance to 1936', MA thesis, University of Cape Town, 1985.

Index

Pietersen, Mr, 50
police, *see* South African Police
Pollsmoor March, 114
Pollsmoor Prison, 74, 110
Portland Cement squatter camp, 113,
    118, 122, 124, 126, 129, 131-136,
    138, 147, 160
President's Council, 97
Prevention of Illegal Squatting Act, 16
Progressive Federal Party, 23, 129,
    137, 142
        Unrest Monitoring Committee,
        136
progressive organisations, 76, 88,
    90, 110-111, 114-118, 120, 123,
    125, 129, 131, 137, 139, 147-148,
    151, 161-163
Public Safety Act, 149

Quakers, 17, 23, 57, 72-73

Red Cross, 135
reform, 28, 33, 39-41, 71, 108, 149,
    153-154, 158-159
refugees, 131, 136-137, 140-142,
    145-146, 153
relief agencies, 135
removals
        threat, 101, 161
rent
        boycott, 103-104
        struggle, 104, 160
Richman, M., 16, 23, 29-30, 32, 34-35,
    38, 48-49, 52, 62
Riekert Commission, 36, 78
roadblocks, 136
Robb, N., 8
Russell, Rev. D., 16

SACLA Clinic, 107, 115, 128-129
Sakela Mr, 44
Samuel, E., 142-143
Sand Dune squatters, 75-77, 80, 94
Save Crossroads Campaign, 22-24
Schreuder, Col. H., 125-126

Security Forces, 103, 113-115, 117-118,
    120, 124-125, 127-128 131-132, 142,
    145, 147, 152
Security Police, *see* South African
    Police
Selani, W., 18
Shangana, J., 137
Siphika, A., 112-113, 122, 125-127,
    135, 141, 149-151
Site C, 111-113, 123, 126, 136, 148,
    150, 153, 161
Sitwaye, F., 123
Sizamile
        committee, 20, 23-25, 45-47, 61,
        63-64
        school, 18, 46, 88
        Soga, W., 83, 106, 110
        South African Broadcasting
            Corporation (SABC), 74
South African Council of Churches
    (SACC), 22
South African Defence Force (SADF),
    29, 113, 138, 140-141, 148
South African Police (SAP), 29, 52,
    80, 85, 100, 107-108, 111, 115, 119,
    123-125, 127-137, 139-142, 144-148,
    151-152, 154, 163
        Security, 52, 125, 134, 136, 152
Soweto Uprising, 17, 24, 83, 109, 158
squatter
        relief, 135
satellite camps, 115, 122, 125, 129,
    131, 135, 138, 140-142 149, 153,
    161-163
St George's Cathedral, 76
State of Emergency, 103-104, 114-115,
    131-132, 141, 146-147, 154-155,
    161-163
Steyn, Judge, 25, 34, 97
Steyn, M., 21
Stock Road, 128
Stuurman, A., 90
Swart, Brig C., 149
Swartklip, 80
Swartzberg, I., 110

Tableview, 72